NARCISSIST

Discover the true meaning of narcissism and how to avoid their mind games, guilt, and manipulation

By

DANIEL ANDERSON

© **Copyright 2018 - All rights reserved.**

The content contained within this book may not be reproduced, duplicated or transmitted without direct written permission from the author or the publisher.

Under no circumstances will any blame or legal responsibility be held against the publisher, or author, for any damages, reparation, or monetary loss due to the information contained within this book. Either directly or indirectly.

Legal Notice:

This book is copyright protected. This book is only for personal use. You cannot amend, distribute, sell, use, quote or paraphrase any part, or the content within this book, without the consent of the author or publisher.

Disclaimer Notice:

Please note the information contained within this document is for educational and entertainment purposes only. All effort has been executed to present accurate, up to date, and reliable, complete information. No warranties of any kind are declared or implied. Readers acknowledge that the author is not engaging in the rendering of legal, financial, medical or professional advice. The content within this book has been derived from various sources. Please consult a licensed professional before attempting any techniques outlined in this book.

By reading this document, the reader agrees that under no circumstances is the author responsible for any losses, direct or indirect, which are incurred as a result of the use of information contained within this document, including, but not limited to, — errors, omissions, or inaccuracies.

TABLE OF CONTENT

CHAPTER 1 BASIC KNOWLEDGE ON NARCISSISM 5
   Narcissism and Its Traits 5
   Self-Love is Not Narcissism! 7
   Narcissism: Ancient and Modern 10
   Narcissism and Today's Society 22

CHAPTER 2 THE SIGNS AND RED FLAGS OF NARCISSISM IN RELATIONSHIPS 35
   Can You Tell if Someone Has a Narcissistic Personality Disorder? 35
   Recognizing the Signs of Narcissistic Personality Disorder 39
   Narcissistic Pointers in Relationships - 8 Signs of Narcissism in Your Partner 41
   "Brattiness" May Be Narcissism 43

CHAPTER 3 HOW TO PREVENT AND AVIOD NARCISSISTIC ABUSE 50
   The Season of the Narcissistic Emotional Abuser 50
   How to Handle Narcissistic Abuse 52
   Narcissistic Individuals Target Your Greatest Fears and Weaknesses 57
   7 Phases of Narcissistic Abuse (and How to Stop It No Matter Where You Are) 60

CHAPTER 4 WHY NARCISSISTIC ABUSE SURVIVOR GETS ADDICTED 66
   What Is Narcissistic Abuse? 66
   7 Signs You've Arrived as a Survivor of Narcissistic Abuse 73
   Forgive or Not Forgive Narcissistic Abuser? 77

CHAPTER 5 TIPS FOR COPING IN RELATIONSHIP WITH NARCISSISTS 85
- Are You in a Relationship With a Narcissist? 85
- What Makes You Vulnerable to a Narcissistic Partner 88
- How to Deal with a Narcissistic Partner 91
- Relationship Tips - How to Manage Love with a Narcissistic Individual 95
- How to Stop Obsessing Over a Narcissistic Relationship 101
- 4 Relationship Tips to Help You Deal with Your Narcissistic Partner 103
- In Love with a Narcissist? Here's Some Great Relationship Advice for You! 108

CHAPTER 6 HEALING AND RECOVERING FROM NARCISSISM AND EMOTIONAL ABUSE . 112
- Discover Your Level of Narcissism 112
- Healing From A Relationship With A Narcissist 115
- Recovery From Narcissistic Abuse - To Get Your Life Back On Track 118
- Emotional Abuse - 8 Steps to Recovery 120
- Best Tips to Recover From Narcissistic Abuse 124

CHAPTER 1

BASIC KNOWLEDGE ON NARCISSISM

Narcissism and Its Traits

Narcissus was a mythological Greek male who looked adoringly at himself in the reflection of a stream and became forever in love with his image. From that mythology, a definition of a type of personality was born...Narcissism. In its extreme, it is known as Narcissistic Personality Disorder (NPD). This type of disorder is characterized by an all-consuming focus on oneself to the exclusion of anyone else.

This person has no regard for anyone's feelings, is without empathy, usually takes advantage of others for personal gain, seeks admiration from all he comes in contact with and is likely to be caught up with the fantasy of his self-importance. Narcissism is more often found in men than women (3 times more men than a woman).

NPD is at the end of the spectrum, and there are many more people with narcissistic traits than those with NPD. However, I will be focusing on NPD in this book.

There are many attributes that can be used to help one to identify a narcissist. Since becoming involved with someone who has this disorder will likely turn out to be a very negative experience it is a good idea to know what to watch for.

He needs to be right all the time. This is part of the inflated ego of the narcissist, never admitting wrongdoing or misjudgment. He will try to manipulate the data and the conversation in such a way as to find fault with everyone but himself.

He exaggerates or lies about accomplishments. This trait is part of the need to feel superior by using grandiose statements to boost his feelings of self-importance.

He expects special treatment wherever he is and whatever the circumstance. This could see as obnoxious or overly pushy behaviour in a restaurant or theatre, as though he deserved a certain "celebrity" status.

He craves admiration or adoration from everyone. If he can't get that need met he may become angry or hostile like some petulant child who can't get his way.

He has no concern for others. He lacks sympathy or empathy and acts as if other people's feelings are not important.

He will often try to dominate a conversation, as though his input were far more valuable than anyone else's.

He tries to manipulate or even brainwash others into believing what he wants them to believe.

He is often envious of others who he sees as celebrated or rich. He also believes others are envious of him, supporting his fantasy that he is more powerful, smarter or even richer than he is.

Self-Love is Not Narcissism!

Not only is self-love not narcissism; unfortunately, narcissists do not know how to begin to love themselves! Keep reading to discover the difference and to learn why self-love is vitally important today.

I have heard people describe narcissists as persons who love themselves - or love themselves too much! Because I was blessed to be taught self-love, I bristle every time I hear that description.

At MayoClinic.com, I found the following definition of narcissistic personality disorder: "Narcissistic personality disorder is a mental disorder in which people have an inflated sense of their importance and a deep need for admiration. They believe that they are superior to others and have little regard for other people's feelings. But behind this mask of ultra-confidence lies a fragile self-esteem, vulnerable to the slightest criticism."

A true narcissist considers himself to be of greater value than others, believing he is entitled to the best of everything. Narcissistic personality disorder should not be confused with healthy self-esteem. Although truly confident people are in touch with their gifts and talents, they do not consider themselves superior.

If self-love is not narcissism, what is it? Self-love is the ability to extend kindness and compassion to yourself. It is the ability to extend kindness and compassion that is sometimes nurturing and other times confrontational. You can be honest with you about motives, intentions, choices, behaviour, and words. Further, it is your ability, to be honest without hurting you over it! I like the way Joseph sums it up; self-love is the willingness to embrace all that we are. The way I sum it up is that self-love is when you give yourself the kind of love, affirmation, and boundaries that you wish your parents had been able to give you.

Many of us were taught as children to forget ourselves in deference to those around us. Some were encouraged to be selfless as a morally right way to be. Others were encouraged to put themselves last because the adults around them were emotionally needy. Surrounded by genuine need, some learned to set their own needs and desires aside.

Of course, selflessness is a good trait. There are problems in the world that would go unsolved without it. The problem for individuals arises when after an extended time of giving selflessly to others; our inner wells of love begin to run dry. When selflessness is part of a dysfunctional relationship, the insecurity driving it undermines other aspects of our outpouring love, causing self-hate to fill that inner well of love.

When we attempt to pour out love and to care without having nurtured love for ourselves, resentment invariably comes to the surface, sabotaging our efforts to love others. Those who have come to depend on our ability to fill them up with love, become frightened and needy when our selflessness begins to dry up. We create a cycle where manipulation and resentment take the place of love and generosity even as we attempt to extend love and generosity.

The answer to this conundrum is simple but challenging! Practising the discipline of self-love will turn it all around, slowly but surely. Not only will you get your love and generosity back. Practising the discipline of self-love will teach you to set boundaries with those who pull on you inappropriately, which is a greater act of love toward others.

The practice of self-love brings us back to facing that old nemesis, Narcissus! Do you remember how Narcissus gazed at his reflection in still water? Well, a good place to begin the practice of self-love is by looking at your own reflection in a mirror and saying to yourself, "I love you," over and over. Repeating it the way you might soothe a child with the words.

The difference between this practice and the myth of Narcissus is when we say, "I love you" to our own reflection in the mirror, we put ourselves in a humble place where we will confront everything we do not like about ourselves. From a wrinkle or hair out of place, to the way we spoke to our spouse last night, to the way we dismissed that irritating person at work, to the motives behind the excess food we ate, etc.; when we make the commitment to say, "I love you," to ourselves, we invariably confront everything we dislike or hate about ourselves.

This is a good thing. It means we get to tame the dragon inside who are trying to consume us before we do more damage to others or ourselves.

Rilke said, "Perhaps all the dragons in our lives are but princesses that are waiting to see us act just once with beauty and courage. Perhaps everything terrible is, in its deepest essence, something helpless that needs our love."

You need your love. You deserve your love. Take a risk today. Risk your inner voice calling you a narcissist and tell you that you love you, unconditionally and unequivocally! Your heart, your inner child, you will be glad you did.

Narcissism: Ancient and Modern

Modern psychology presents the importance of narcissism, self-absorption, in the construction of mental illness. Evidence of narcissism indicates mental instability. Ambitious individuals have, from this perspective, damaged psyches. Freud saw Narcissism as a default mechanism, energy that should have been going outward being turned inward with destructive effects. It can be observed, if one chooses to do so, in some psychotic and sociopathic conditions. This part will consider the one-dimensional nature of such an approach, and how the Narcissus and Echo myths, utilized by Freud, demonstrate wider cultural truths and that the insights of ancient people were deeper more compelling than those of recent modern thinkers. It suggests that the modern belief in healthy relationships as evidence of psychic health and unimpeded emotional growth is absurd.

The book will look at the Narcissus and Echo myths, considering their relevance to the Ancient Athenians, the Roman poet Ovid, as well as to psychoanalysis, critiquing the views of Melanie Klein, Alice Miller (who rejected psychoanalysis) and the Object Relations' School and examine what can be learned of differing cultural perspectives on human behaviour, and what light this throws upon psychoanalysis, exploring the contradictions and similarities of the different approaches, placing the psychoanalytical understanding of the myth in its cultural context. Psychoanalysis is in this view, only another cultural interpretation.

Both psychiatry and psychoanalysis insist on the differentiation of human beings according to largely subjective categories, so ambition, success, exemplary achievement is re-classified within various terms denoting pathological behaviour. This book rejects such ideas.

The Ancient Athenian Concept of Human Nature,

With the evolution of the Greek polis or city-state, there existed a tension between ideas of civilisation, civilised nature and the natural world. Athenian men, as citizens of the polis, distinct from women, symbolised the concepts of reason and rationality. The perfect expression of humankind was a man who lived within a city and was part of a city community. The notion of an individual set apart from a city was not understood, viewed as an aberration or as a primitive form of consciousness.

Homosexual relationships were normal in most ancient Greek societies during adolescence, usually between a younger and an older man. Male romantic passion was reserved for their sex rather than towards members of the opposite sex. The friendship between men was prized above all. Lastly, in Athens, there was a sharp division between public life, a male domain, and private life, a female domain.

The Attia of Flower Myths. (Metamorphosis)

'And in its stead, they found a flower-behold/White petals clustered round a cup of gold.'

There were different versions of the myth in ancient Greece, used and developed mainly by Hellenistic poets, serving a didactic purpose. The myth may originally have concerned the worship of Eros. Ancient Greek myths which detailed metamorphosis into flowers usually had an erotic connotation, linking youth and beauty, often telling of boys dying young with their virginity intact and their metamorphosis into beautiful, useful plants. The metamorphosis stories, while erotic, do not end in sexual fulfilment and fertility. According to Forbes Irving, the metamorphosis of humans or deities reflects human development, or in the case of transformation into plants, evidence of early cults. It involves the primitive side of human nature before socialization and urban life.

Narcissus is warned that he will die young unless he learns to know himself. Such knowledge comes from sharing in a relationship. Narcissus sees his reflection in a pool, falls in love with it, and slowly dies, transforming into a flower. He did not understand that his image was his. He did not, therefore, know himself. The flower is a narcotic, suggesting the transformational effects of such plants and the subsequent self-absorption. The point is, by expressing fertility a youth becomes a man, that is a citizen of a polis. Ovid's myth concerns the essential value of human development, growing sexually and emotionally.

To the Greeks, the myth also expresses the problem of excess. Too much beauty meant that Narcissus was competing with the gods and had therefore to die. Also, the natural world was unable to tolerate too much wealth, luck or beauty and destroys it. The same responses can be found in our world with the sometimes hidden anger towards celebrities and the more fortunate. For Klein excess encourages the envy of others. Narcissus suffered not only from an excess of beauty but also from his virginity, in the latter offending Eros, according to Bremmer.

Echo. 'Her love endures and grows on grief.'

It is likely the first connection between Narcissus and Echo was made by Hellenistic poets, not Ovid.

Narcissus was unable to love Echo, a nymph of trees and springs. He rejected her, and she faded away until only her voice remained. I suggest that Echo personifies bestial sex through her relationship with Pan, with whom she had a son, and through being a woman. In ancient Athens women symbolized irrationality. They were associated with nature, the uncivilized part of humankind and unbridled lust.

The destructive relationship between Narcissus and Echo may, therefore, have reflected the tensions between civilized man and nature. Narcissus declares in Ovid: 'Keep your arms from me/Be off! I'll die before I yield to you.' This may not simply be youthful arrogance. It certainly looks like that stage when a youth becomes a functioning sexual being or symbolic of exclusive homosexuality. Echo's decline into a voice repeating the last word of other's sentences may symbolize the suppression of Athenian women and their lack of involvement in the polis.

The Athenian males' suppression of women may have had its roots in their upbringing. Exclusively cared for by their mothers until adolescence they were then brought up by their fathers and taught to despise and fear women. This presents an alternative to Klein's view that the primitive emotions of 'envy and gratitude' stemmed from reactions to the primary object. The mother. Athenian's present such emotions as subject to ritualised behaviour, motivated by community drives. The primitive emotions envisaged by Klein would have been modified for use by the community, aiding the polis, as a community run by men with an emphasis on militarism, debate and public work, with all the intellectual contracts of rationality and reason that ensued.

The myth may reflect the tensions of the time within society between gender and the nature of erotic love. It is thus inappropriate to attach individual psychological positions to Narcissus and Echo. The two stories concern reciprocity, which obsessed with ancient Greeks. The relationships ancient Athenians enjoyed with their wives carried less emotional value than in the present day. The sex act between men and women was practical, assuring women lacked influence in society. In ancient Athens, a man's individuality was expressed as a component of the community, not as modern-day individuality. Narcissus' metamorphosis returns him to the natural world, where, because of the medicinal powers of the plant he becomes more useful to society. The narcotic qualities of the flower express, I believe, fertility rather than obsession or addiction.

The Myth According io Ovid:

Perry: 'True perceptions cannot be distinguished from false ones, for every perception that is true, there is one resembling it that is false.'

Ovid composed in the Classical Tradition, meaning he imitated and referenced Greek and Roman writers before him. His poetry is didactic in the manner of Callimachus, the Hellenistic poet, and Metamorphoses debates the nature of literary form, reality and the materialistic philosophy of Lucretius. Ovid changes the myth from a homosexual to heterosexual account.

I will look at Ovid's rendering of the myth of Narcissus to find if he agrees with or throws light onto the Freudian interpretation with his focus upon individual character as understood through sexual nature. I will examine Ovid's understanding of love, reality, experience, gender, paradox and fate. Certainly, Narcissus' predicament reflects for Ovid Plato's views of knowledge and reality.

Ovid questions the validity of perception through love and permanence of gender. Tiresias, who foretold the future, was for a brief period transformed into a woman, experiencing sex as both a man and a woman. By so doing, the unfixed nature of sexuality was emphasised. Freud sees sex as fundamental in the development of human character, interpreting the objective world through sexual drives, childhood trauma, memory and ego. For Ovid sexuality concerns the ontological nature of reality. He perceives human sexuality as more fluid and less liable to categorisation than Freud.

Narcissus' love for his reflection concerns for Ovid the deceptiveness of love and shows how falling in love can distort reality, confusing boundaries between subject and object. This perhaps more reflects Klein's views on 'the defences of the early ego', whereby reality is structured by the early development of the self through its relation to an object. Subject and object become confused.

Narcissus' nature in Ovid, transfixed like a stone by his reflection, suggests his character before metamorphoses according to Forbes Irving. This is not about the 'tragedy of the loss of self', as Miller believes, denied by the effects of grandiosity from adapting to the needs and desires of others, but about his ability to deceive. He is deceived by the fluctuating nature of reality ('You see a phantom of a mirrored shape') and the demands of his fate.

For Ovid, Echo serves as a further example of the insubstantiality of reality, rather than the individual, as understood in modern psychological theories, caught within a dependency relationship upon another. Echo reflects vocally in the same fashion as water reflects Narcissus' image. Also, it may concern how language forms an identity, prefiguring Freud's grabbing with the matter. As with the Greeks from whom Ovid took many of his ideas and literary forms, the paradoxes' of reality contained within the myth are transformed into something of greater general use.

Narcissus and Psychoanalysis:

Freud believed that narcissism is the 'libidinal complement to the egoism of the instinct of self-preservation.'

In this section, I aim to show that psychoanalysis represents a shift in perspective about our understanding of objective reality from an emphasis on the external world and humankind' relationship to it to an emphasis on an internal world, with a corresponding shift in the understanding of reality and experience. Subjective reality became thereby a consequence of individual experience, and splitting of reality becomes apparent. Individuals relate to only part of the world rather than the world as a whole. The later concepts of Freud (Civilization and Its Discontents) merely acknowledge the importance of external reality, which is a commonsense strategy, but not its part in constructing objective reality. He perceives the external world as providing stimuli for the structuring of reality through individual impulses. This encourages the view that individual sexual drives or ego create events.

Such a perspective can be observed in Klein's views on the child's internalization of external objects and the introjections of the 'good internalized breast and the bad devouring breast' which underlines her understanding of Narcissism. The myth shows Narcissus metamorphosed into an element of the greater world, becoming a flower of beauty and medicinal qualities. In psychoanalysis, individuals become defined through their relationships with others, not through relationships with ideas, God, or the greater world. In object relations (Winnicott and Kohut) this is often reduced to a relationship with the primary object, the mother. It is a lesser world.

The Narcissistic Personality: 'so long as he suffers, he ceases to love.'

Freud perceives the self-absorption of Narcissus as primary narcissism, the 'libidinal cathexis of the ego', and preceding cathexis of the primary object, the individual's first nurse, and an inability to properly relate to others if continued into adulthood. They could not relate to or love others. Freud perceived these characteristics within psychotic personalities, who appeared unable to exhibit interest in the external world but showed interest only in themselves. He also saw it in paranoiacs and homosexuals who may have identified with the mother when children. Narcissus' rejection of intimacy in Ovid's telling of the myth is not, according to Freud, about the mutable quality of reality but the individual's creation of an ego-ideal that results in 'overvaluation' of their qualities and capacities.

Freud's observations seem to have been exclusively connected with the apparent self-absorption of psychically damaged individuals within his practice, or those suffering addiction. This one-dimensional characteristic may have been exaggerated by Freud due to his limited exposure to the ordinary activities of his parents. His relationship with his patients was limited to their relationship with themselves, with others through their interpretation, failing to invest them with a valid intellectual life or allowing any influences to bear beyond the narrow focus of their sexual and emotional lives and those of others acquainted with them. The Narcissist of Freud appears attached to a smaller, sterile world, bound by individual egoism or libidinal drives compared to Ovid's Narcissus. Freud's early association of Narcissism and homosexuality may have had its roots in the specific delineation of gender attributes of his period.

Klein: 'the mean and grudging breast.'

Beautiful Narcissus, for the ancient Athenians, was the envy of others. That decided his fate. Klein sees such narcissism as evidence of the sufferer's envy. The world is perceived from the inside out, the individual born with an un-cohesive ego and temperamental predisposition restructuring the world according to early experiences with a primary object. This can be altered through the later Oedipus period and the depressive position. For Klein, the destructive envy of Narcissism begins early, and, the prime object of envy, as a consequence of dependency and subsequent fear of annihilation, is the mother's breast. The mother becomes the bad object; a function of the baby in the paranoid-schizoid position before the baby has a perception of the mother's being a separate object. Fairbairn appears to view the mother as determining the development of psychic problems. The death of Narcissus' putative lover, himself, and Echo's fate, from this perspective, is part of the envious destructive quality of narcissism. The 'scooping out, sucking dry, and devouring' of 'the breast'. The destruction of the creativity the Narcissist envies in others. This envy prevents the proper development of object-cathexis, focusing upon a mature love object. The baby's ego is early split between itself and the primary object, which is usually the mother.

For the Athenians, Narcissus and Echo represented the tensions specific to the polis, their relationship to the erotic, homosexual inclinations they owned, and to the journey of early life that culminated in an assumption of communal responsibilities. Childhood was part of that journey, regarded as a preparation for the real business of life, serving the community. This youth did at nineteen when they were expected to fight for the city-state. The years with their mothers were to ensure preservation. Learning began under the auspices of fathers. The traumas itemised by Freud and Klein would, assuming they exist, have been subsumed into the drives of the whole community. The early years of manhood were considered of far greater importance than childhood, an unproductive period of dependency. Children were not useful. Narcissus occupied the point between unproductively and usefulness.

Ovid dealt with the complexities of reality, the fashion that love, erotic intimacy, reflects that complexity. He understood the world intellectually and would probably have dismissed Miller's refutation of intellectuality as a source of self-knowledge on the basis that reality is not determined by feelings or individual histories. Freud, Klein, Miller and the Object Relation's School appear to have believed this disturbing notion. People's relationships are perhaps a reflection of different notions of reality and do not construct it. Both the ancient Athenians and Ovid emphasized the drives of communities and ideas beyond themselves. Psychoanalysis and Psychiatry view drove, high accomplishing individuals as exhibiting evidence of Narcissistic personality disorders when their drives are more complex than self-absorption and often informed by intellectuality which neither of the above considers a formative force.

Object Relations' School

This mainly British version of psychology views relationships as the goal of human existence, and all other endeavours as distractions from this goal. These other endeavours, creating a business empire, writing books, other less agreeable activities, were put down to self-grandiosity (see Miller, 2001). Neither the ancient Athenians nor Ovid would have understood this notion. The Athenians would have considered it shocking. While they would have appreciated the association with hubris, the alternative focus on relationships would have horrified them. Ovid would probably have viewed it as an absurd trivialization of existence.

In societies where the individual was an expression of greater ideals, the polis or Imperial Rome and its mission, perceiving life as being about the pursuit of healthy relationships would have been treasonable or childish. Historical drives, for at least the elite, took the place of individual drives. Sexuality was not necessarily connected to individual happiness, conceived of as either a deeply serious matter (Athens) or connected to power and the state (Rome), it was far too important for that. Object Relations foisting of later individual development on the mother alone appears like an assertion of masculinity as a reaction to Britain's loss of Imperial and political power.

You are viewing individual drive, intellectuality and choice as simply evidence of a damaged psyche, controls and limits self-expression, individuality and creativity. It was, and remains, a dangerous step forward — the accompanying celebration of relationships sanctions conformity and mediocrity.

Narcissism and Today's Society

The subject of 'Narcissism' has intrigued us for many decades, but social scientists now claim that it has become a "modern epidemic". The term 'Narcissism' originated more than 2000 years ago when Ovid wrote the 'Legend of Narcissus', which tells the story of a beautiful Greek hunter, Narcissus, who, one day, sees his reflection in a pool of water and falls in love with it. He becomes obsessed with his beauty and is unable to leave his reflected image until he dies. The concept of Narcissism was first introduced by the famous psychoanalyst, Dr Sigmund Freud's essay 'On Narcissism'. He popularized this new concept through his work on the 'ego' and its relation to the outside world. Narcissism can be defined as the pursuit of gratification from vanity or egotistic admiration of one's attributes. The 'American Psychiatry Association' has classified this as 'Narcissistic Personality Disorder' (NPD).

Narcissism lies on a continuum from healthy to pathological. Healthy narcissism is part of normal human functioning. It represents the required self - love and confidence based on real achievements and the ability to overcome setbacks. But, narcissism becomes a problem when one becomes excessively preoccupied with the self and seeks complete admiration and attention, with complete disregard for others' feelings. Lack of satisfaction of this need leads to substance abuse and major depressive disorders. In adolescents, this causes 'Substance Dependency Disorder' (SDD) - they display overt narcissistic and prosaically behaviours, which show a connection between self - centeredness and addiction. These substances include sedatives like alcohol, psychedelics and hallucinogens like marijuana and LSD, stimulants like cocaine, narcotics like opium, heroin, and morphine, and anti-anxiety drugs like Xanax.

"Narcissists unconsciously deny an unstated and intolerably poor self - image through inflation. They turn themselves into glittering figures of immense grandeur, surrounded by psychologically impenetrable walls. The goal of this self - deception is to be impervious to greatly feared external criticism, and to their rolling sea of doubts." This is how Elan Golomb describes NPD, in her book 'Trapped in the Mirror'. The narcissists fail to achieve intimacy with anyone as they view other people like items in a vending machine, and uses them to serve their own needs, never being able to acknowledge that others might have their feelings too.

Narcissism is filled with irony and paradox, whether as a character trait or as a clinical disease. Emily Levine says, "I thought Narcissism was about self - love till someone told me there is a flip - side to it... it is unrequited self - love." It must be remembered that Narcissus weeps to find out that his image does not return his love. This indicates that a loving engagement with the self does not, and cannot, come from putting on lofty airs, acting with self - satisfied arrogance or being obsessed with assorted fantasies of ideal brilliance or beauty. Healthy, non - egotistical self - love arises from an unconditional acceptance of the self, without having to declare superiority over others. Deep down, the narcissists know, albeit unconsciously, that they are not really what they project. One of their central defences is to endlessly project onto others the very flaws and fears that they are unable or unwilling, to allow into awareness. They are critical of others' shortcomings but completely blind to their own - their self - love must be seen as an illusion, a spectacular triumph of self - deception. They can only love their false, idealized self - a mirage that cannot possibly return the fantasy-laden love. Their flawed self, hidden beneath their outward bravado, remains locked up and placed in permanent exile. And, to continuously safeguard themselves from a reality that so frequently contradicts their grandiose assumptions and pretensions, they are forced to employ a massive defence stratagem, with extraordinary rigidity.

Although very few of us are diagnosed with NPD, almost all of us are guilty of sharing certain narcissistic tendencies. So, Todd Solondz says, "Narcissism and self - deception are survival mechanisms without which many of us might just jump off the bridge." For true narcissists, the defences are necessary to compensate for their ego deficits and reduce feelings of shame. Without them, they might result in a state of suicidal depression; for, narcissists do not like themselves - the more they boast and demean others, they are more likely to cover up for their deeper, largely hidden feelings of inferiority and lack of love. Blinded by their idealized self - image, they try to project themselves as gifted, exceptional and unique - that in turn makes them egotistical and arrogant. According to TS Eliot, "... half the harm that is done in this world is due to people who want to feel important. They don't mean to harm but the harm [that they cause] does not interest them. Or they do not see it, or they justify it because they are absorbed in the endless struggle to think well of themselves." This shows a distinction between narcissists who are malevolent and those who simply lack concern of how their behaviour might adversely affect others. It is yet another way of gaining attention to their supreme self - absorption, which makes it impossible for them to identify with others' feelings.

Kurt Cobain says, "I don't care what you think unless it is about me." This shows the narcissist's indifference to the outer world unless it specifically relates to them. They are completely incapable of a genuine interest in others' matters unless they are needed for the former's assertion of superiority. Narcissists are also great con - artists; after all, they always succeed in deceiving themselves. It becomes particularly painful when they suffer from memory loss, when, they lose out parts of the person they love the most. In general, a narcissist "devours people, consumes their output, and casts the empty, wreathing shells aside", says Sam Vaknin. Hate is a complement of fear, and the narcissists like being feared - it provides them with an intoxicating sensation of omnipotence. The difference between Narcissism and self - love is a matter of depth. Narcissus falls in love not with the self, but with an image or reflection of the self, with the persona, the mask. Narcissists see themselves through the eyes of others, changes their lifestyle and behaviour and expression of feelings, according to others' admiration. Narcissism is voluntary blindness, an agreement not to look beneath the surface. Oscar Wilde says, "To love oneself is the beginning of a life - long romance" - this notion of self - love leans towards the pathological and the autoerotic as well.

Prof. Jean Twenge differentiates narcissism from the idea of self - esteem. One high in self - esteem, values individual achievements, but they also value their relationships and caring for others. Contrarily, narcissists miss out on valuing and caring their relationships, as they lack empathy. Prof. Twenge and Keith Campbell, a specialist on Narcissism, joined hands to investigate whether people born in more recent generations score higher against Narcissism measures than in previous generations. The tool they used to assess their subjects is the 'Narcissistic Personality Inventory' (NPI), created in 1988. It is the most widely used measure of Narcissism in social - psychological research, where a 40 item forced - choice version is the one most commonly employed. Following Freud's and Kohut's theories, individuals would be diagnosed clinically as patients of NPD, if they fulfil the following criteria:

A. Grandiose sense of self - importance or uniqueness

B. Preoccupation with fantasies of unlimited success, power, brilliance, beauty, or ideal love

C. Exhibitionism

D. Cold indifference of marked feelings of rage, inferiority, shame, humiliation or emptiness in response to criticism, the indifference of others or defeat

E. At least, two of the following characteristic disturbances in interpersonal relationships:

I. Entitlement - the expectation of special favour without assuming reciprocal responsibilities

II. Interpersonal exploits

III. Relationships that characteristically alternate between the two extremes of over idealisation and devaluation

IV. Lack of empathy

F. Vulnerability to shame, rather than guilt

G. Denial of remorse or gratitude

In this regard, reference can be made to Hotchkiss's 'Seven Deadly Sins of Narcissism', which include shamelessness, magical thinking, arrogance, envy, entitlement, exploitation, bad boundaries.

The 'narcissistic dilemma' is seen when, being criticized, the narcissists show themselves pitifully incapable of retaining any emotional poise or receptivity. But, these disturbed individuals also display an abnormally developed capacity to criticize others. Their dilemma is that the rigidity of their defences, their inability ever to let their guard down, even among their closest people, guarantees that they will never get what they most need, which, unfortunately, they are themselves oblivious to. People are never born narcissist; it is powerful environmental influences that make them so. Being neglected and ignored, or constantly disparaged or berated by parents in childhood, they form unrealistically high standards of behaviour. Unable to meet up to their parents' unreasonable, perfectionist expectations, they create an imaginary "ideal self" that could receive parental acceptance, even adulation, which they yearn for. The main elements of narcissism are narcissistic supply, narcissistic rage and narcissistic injury, and narcissistic abuse. Narcissism can be of various types, and its causes are not yet well - known. Inherited genetic defects are thought to be responsible in some cases, along with environmental factors:

1. Childhood abuse or neglect

2. Excessive parental pampering

3. The unrealistic expectation of parents

4. Sexual promiscuity

5. Cultural influences

A study shows the changes in levels of Narcissism over the past few decades, among the college-going students, i.e. the youth; it is seen rampant in the society of the USA today, because these youths are the future leaders, and Narcissism is very harmful to the society as a whole and can cause failure in academic and other endeavours. Twenge and Campbell surveyed American institutions from 1979 - 2006 and found an upward shift in scores on the NPI, meaning that, now the average college student embraces narcissistic tendencies more than their counterparts, two decades ago. The rise in Narcissism in the American population might be because now, from a young age, Americans are taught that they are very special and unique, that in turn increases their self - esteem. Extroversion and assertion are the key factors of Narcissism. It is also due to the large emphasis on materialism and wealth, with a focus on an individual's pleasure and success, in the current American society.

Today, Narcissism has gripped the entire world, as indicated by the rapid change in society that occurred during the industrial and post-industrial times. The past few decades have witnessed a societal shift from a commitment to the collective to a focus on the individual or self. Here comes in the 'self - esteem movement' which became the key to success in life. The parents tried to "confer" self - esteem upon their children rather than allowing them to achieve it through hard work. The rise of individualism and the decline in social norms that accompanied the modernization of society led to a shift from the concept of what is best for the others and family to what is best for "me". The commercial world with a total focus on wealth and fame created an "empty self, shorn of social meaning". Today, the generation of young adults - the 'Generation Y' - also known as the 'Millenials' and 'Generation Me', comprising of individuals born between 1975 - 1995, are condemned for being narcissistic, selfish, self - entitled, and having unrealistic expectations from life.

The rise in technology and the advancement of immensely popular social networking sites like Facebook, Twitter, Instagram, MySpace, YouTube have changed the way we now spend our leisure time and communicate with others. Internet addiction is a new area of study in mental health, and many researchers show that addiction to Facebook, Twitter is strongly linked to narcissistic behaviour and low self - esteem. The notion that the current generation is increasingly becoming narcissistic, as a product of the "like effect" (a theory where the number of 'likes' on social media produces greater self - esteem) has been widely debated. This effect creates negative self - esteem contrary to egotism due to modern youths constantly comparing the quantity of 'likes' or the quality of a picture to that of another. The ego can never be satisfied with an increasing number of 'likes'. Also, the total control over one's perception of social media allows modern youth to see an unrealistic, distorted image that they will compare themselves to. Thus, regular posting of 'selfies' on social media promotes Narcissism, that is a cry of ego - satisfaction. Social networking sites are believed to be outlets for narcissistic expression, and Gen Y, aged between 17 - 21 years, are particularly vulnerable to its negative effects. Lucy Clyde says, "If you are a narcissist, you are looking for a positive reflection of yourself, the world is your mirror, and you are constantly looking for affirmation. For this reason, you're probably curating your own life very heavily on social media."

Named 'Word of the Year' in 2013 by the Oxford English Dictionary, the term "selfie" has become very common among all teens and young adults, in today's technological era. A "selfie" is defined as "a photograph that one has taken of oneself, typically one taken by a smartphone or a webcam, and shared via social media". For Gen Y, taking selfies and posting them on social media has become inevitable parts of daily living, promoting Narcissism. Millennials, aged 18 - 33 years, are hyper-connected with little awareness or concern for the others. "Generation Me", today, is a victim of the 'Selfie Syndrome' - they post, tag and comment on self - portraits, believing that others are interested in their daily activities, and they want to tell others what they are doing. Selfies symbolize that shamelessly flaunting your Narcissism is trendy; if you put an inspirational quote under your selfie, no one can see your Narcissism. A selfie a day keeps insecurities away - "constantly taking selfies will not make you prettier; may you someday find someone to love you as much as your selfies indicate you love yourself." Today, the confidence level is measured by "a selfie with no filter". Never before has a generation so diligently recorded themselves, accomplishing so little - "if you could take selfies of your souls, would you find it attractive enough to post?"

It seems those people who constantly post selfies must not own mirrors like the rest of us; but again, mirrors should not be taken too seriously, as one's true reflection is in his heart. Increase in Narcissism pose a threat to the emotional and psychological health of the youth - it results in self - enhancement and self - promotion, preventing them from establishing lasting intimate relationships. Also, they tend to be prone to respond to violent and aggressive behaviour after being criticized. Online relationships may appeal more to narcissists, who are otherwise unable to, or unwilling, to form meaningful relations that demand any time or emotional attachment. The increase of smartphones and many new sophisticated gadgets allow people to access social media very easily, contributing to widespread Narcissism. Managing and revising one's online profile content is a vital aspect of the youth's online identity and "e - personality". Social networking sites give narcissistic individuals the chance to keep the focus of their profile's content solely on themselves. By this, they post status updates, comments and photos that depict only themselves, and not others, perpetuating their selfish nature. The online profiles allow them to achieve a type of social identity that they wish to portray, through exaggeration of certain character traits and present a persona that they believe is appealing to the world, at large.

Lack of empathy for others causes a preoccupation with the Gen Y's frustrated selves and emotional distresses, while growing up - they go out of their houses, but focused on themselves only, taking selfies - and thus, can never completely come out of their selves. They lose out on moral values and find it difficult to come out of their fears. The increasing demand for plastic surgeries, worldwide, to look better in the eyes of others, is also an unfortunate consequence of the rise of Narcissism. They always remain emotionally and spiritually unfulfilled, hungry for a nebulous something they cannot even conceive, and project a constant detachment in all relationships, even in the most intimate ones.

Treatment of 'Narcissistic Personality Disorder' (NPD) is possible through psychotherapy, or talk - therapy. But Narcissism has certain beneficial effects too. It has a fundamental connection with leadership, as both notions have the common factors - dominance, extroversion, confidence and power. Because of these, narcissists become good and successful leaders, provoked by their desire for self - assertion, glory and power. But today, individualism is co-related to materialism and Narcissism. So, together, the world's Narcissism is huge - the collective Narcissism results in the destruction of the planet. Together, we are wiping out one species after another from this world, fuelled by consumerism and our growing self -

importance. Our Narcissism may eventually turn out to be our Nemesis, in the end.

CHAPTER 2

THE SIGNS AND RED FLAGS OF NARCISSISM IN RELATIONSHIPS

Can You Tell if Someone Has a Narcissistic Personality Disorder?

It is not easy to tell whether or not someone has a Narcissistic Personality Disorder.

However, you may find many telling signs of a Narcissistic Personality Disorder when reading about its symptoms and behaviours. One of the first indicators of a person with Narcissistic Personality Disorder is that they have a larger-than-life personality or a grandiose sense of themselves. They often are braggarts who are always holding onto the belief of others being jealous of them. But in reality, it is quite the opposite. They are the ones who, because they have such low self-esteem, are jealous of others. A common trait in someone who has Narcissism is excessive negativity to constructive criticism. Their ego identities are so fragile criticism is often unbearable for them. In response, they often put others down to build themselves up. The first sign of someone who feels intensely insecure is acting as though others are inferior to them. It is common to label this type of person as having a superiority complex. But again it is the feelings and emotions of not being good enough that fuels their self-serving behaviours.

People with Narcissistic Personality Disorder expect others to work with them to achieve their hopes, goals and dreams regardless of how unrealistic or unattainable those goals are. People with Narcissistic Personality Disorder are insecure and have low self-esteem even if they do not appear that way. Outwardly they are usually perceived as being insensitive and unemotional. As a result, they alienate people and will often have negative relationships with people in both their professional and personal lives.

There is treatment for people who have Narcissistic Personality Disorder, once these symptoms have been detected. To get a Narcissist to admit that he has a problem is very difficult. You would have to work very hard at attaining their acceptance and trust to be able to bring them to this point of their journey. That is why it is more helpful and effective to study about Narcissistic Personality Disorder and educate yourself about how you can change your role, which may well be as a Codependent, in your relationship with a Narcissist. Relationship experts on NPD will help you learn the skills and behaviours you need to adapt to change the dynamics of your relationship with a Narcissist.

Signs of Narcissism

At certain times, we all have narcissistic tendencies. We want our way, we like to be admired for our looks, body or brain and we react negatively to criticism. In a nutshell, within limits, those very traits can be relatively normal. It's important to note, however, that there are extremely unhealthy levels of the narcissistic personality. These high levels of narcissism will take out the innocent and the weak of heart before they can even realize what hit them.

Since someone with Narcissistic Personality Disorder (NPD) doesn't normally wear a sign around their neck, how do you spot them?

- According to the Mayo Clinic, narcissistic symptoms may include:
- The belief that you're superior to others
- An exaggerated fantasy of power, success, status and attractiveness
- Exaggerating your achievements
- Lack of empathy
- Using others to get your way in business, relationships or other aspects of day-to-day life
- Setting unrealistic goals
- Appearing tough-minded/unemotional
- Difficulty keeping healthy and lasting relationships
- The appearance of over-confidence and or arrogance
- Monopolization of conversations (constantly interrupting)
- An attitude of entitlement
- A 'look at me, look at me' attitude

There are several very big clues as to if someone you're in a relationship with is a narcissist. Since in the narcissist's mind they are ultimately more important than others, you can detect narcissistic personality traits by their extreme self-centeredness, manipulation tactics and lack of empathy toward others. Narcissists rarely feel guilt or shame for their behaviours and often place the blame for what they've said or done on someone else (projection); i.e. 'It's your fault I did that. If you hadn't done that, I wouldn't have responded that way.'

A word of caution: People with NPD can be very charming, but are also very hazardous to your emotional well-being. They and are constantly looking for their next "victim" or "narcissistic supply source". The narcissistic supply source is someone who will feed their ego and tell them how wonderful they are, how intelligent they are, that they're a GREAT employee, lover or spouse, etc. The narcissist tells you how hot they look, how in shape they are or how much they're going to make on their next big deal (usually one of many fantasies they wish were real). In essence, everything is about them. Once the narcissist has obtained what they need from you, they'll dispose of your relationship to them (whether they're married to you or not) and leave you wondering what you ever did to make them love you one moment and discard you the next.

Additionally, most people with NPD also have a problem with at least one addiction. For some its drugs, for some it's alcohol, and for other's, it's some sort sexual addiction. Regardless of which one it is, all are extremely dangerous to not only the narcissist but those in closest relationship to them as well.

Recognizing the Signs of Narcissistic Personality Disorder

Narcissistic Personality Disorder is distinguished by a long duration pattern of grandiosity (either in delusion or real-world conduct), an overwhelming wish for admiration, and generally an absolute lack of concern toward others.

People with this sickness typically think that they are of paramount relevance in everyone's life or to anyone they connect with.

A particular person with this particular problem could very well whine about a clumsy waitresses "rudeness" or "ignorance" or end a medical-related evaluation giving a condescending evaluation of the medical profession.

In layman terms, a person with this disorder may be described just as a "narcissist" or as somebody with "narcissism." Both of these terms largely refer to anybody with a narcissistic personality disorder.

Signs of Narcissistic Personality Disorder

For anyone to be identified as having a narcissistic personality they need to match 5 or more of the following symptoms:

Is obsessed with fantasies of inexhaustible achievement, authority, splendour, attractiveness, or perfect love.

Boasts a grandiose feeling of self-importance (e.g., exaggerates accomplishments and skills, wants to be recognized as exceptional without having commensurate achievements)

Thinks that he or she is "extraordinary" and unique and can only be understood by, or should associate with, other unique or high-status men and women (or establishments)

Will require an excessive amount of appreciation.

Is exploitative of other people, e.g., will take advantage of other folks to gain his or her ends.

Has an incredibly strong feeling of entitlement, e.g., unreasonable expectations of specifically favourable treatment or instant concurrence with his or her expectations.

Is short of empathy, e.g., is reluctant to recognize or identify using the emotions and needs of others.

Frequently will show egotistic, haughty behaviours or conduct.

Is usually envious of other people or thinks that others are envious of him or her.

A narcissistic personality disorder is a lot more prevalent in males as compared to women and is particularly believed to develop in much less than 1 per cent of the normal population.

Similar to most personality disorders, narcissistic personality disorder nearly always probably will reduce in seriousness with age, with a lot of people struggling with a couple of the most significant indicators and symptoms once they're inside the Forties or 50s.

Exactly how is Narcissism Diagnosed?

Personality problems like narcissistic personality disorder are typically clinically determined by a qualified psychological wellness expert, for example, a psychologist or psychiatrist.

Household physicians and common practitioners are often not properly trained or well-equipped to create this type of mental health diagnosis

A diagnosis for narcissistic personality disorder is normally made by a mental health specialist evaluating your signs or symptoms and life history with all those listed here.

They're going to decide whether your signs or symptoms met the criteria required for a personality disorder diagnosis.

Treatment of Narcissism.

Proper treatment of narcissistic personality issues almost always will involve long-term psychotherapy with a therapist that has expertise in treating this kind of personality disorder.

Narcissistic Pointers in Relationships - 8 Signs of Narcissism in Your Partner

Relationships have their challenges for everyone. With effort and commitment, two reasonably balanced and emotionally healthy individuals can forge a relationship that is mutually supportive and fulfilling. However, there is a segment of the population that is hard wired with personality disorders. Narcissism is a disorder that often drives the affected individual to act in ways that are very destructive to intimate relationships. The non-disordered partner is often left feeling bewildered and hurt by his or her narcissistic partner's behaviour.

Affairs are extremely painful and shocking for many partners who find out that their partner has not been faithful. While a relationship can survive an affair if both partners recommit and establish excellent communication and accountability, there are instances where affairs can be a sign of more than just an issue in the relationship of origin. A segment of our population is afflicted with a personality disorder, and a common disorder of this type is narcissism. Sometimes, affairs can be an indicator, along with other criteria, of the presence of narcissism in an individual. While only a licensed mental health professional can diagnose narcissism, it can be helpful to know what you are looking for.

Here are eight signs that your partner's affairs could be a deeper sign of narcissism:

1. Poor behavioural control and a tendency toward impulsive behaviour. This can lead to addictions or compulsive sexual behaviours.

2. Lacking in empathy. The narcissist cannot put him or herself in another person's shoes. This leads to acts that appear callous and selfish.

3. An inflated and exaggerated sense of self-worth. Your partner may brag about accomplishments and build them up past their real merit.

4. The sense of entitlement. Your partner might act as if he or she deserves special treatment, and ought to know and associate with others who are special. Often, there is a haughtiness in attitude and a sense of superiority present.

5. A willingness to exploit others for his or her benefit.

6. Jealousy toward others. Your partner might even become enraged at the successes of others, upset that attention is being paid toward anyone else.

7. Needs extreme amounts of admiration from others. This source of admiration is termed "narcissistic supply," and is much like a drug that the narcissist craves.

8. Thinks in ideal terms, such as "perfect" love, beauty, and power. You may be perceived as ideal for some time, then discarded and considered worthless with nothing in between.

"Brattiness" May Be Narcissism

Would you know a Narcissist if you met one? You will find them around your town, on the sports field, and even in your own home. You probably know many kids who you consider to be 'bratty.' Don't expect their parents to do anything about their bad behaviour because the brats I am talking about are now adults — big adult brats, but not necessarily grown-ups.

What causes narcissism? Narcissistic Personality Disorder, that's what. Do you remember that girl at school who stole things, or started rumours (about those least able to defend themselves) but always got away with it because she always charmed or connived her way out of any situation? We all remember kids like that, don't we? One of the hallmarks of a narcissist is blaming others.

If you ever wonder what happens to brats who turn into adults before ever learning good social skills, well ...With a good education they may end up in charge of other people's resources, and possibly run an otherwise healthy company into the ground, or cause a nation's financial ruin. The less educated narcissist men; the ones who use their charm and manipulation to work the system are more likely to end up in jail. Narcissistic women, once they are too old to seduce and exploit men any longer, typically end up dying alone; rejected and despised by all.

Brats bring their narcissism and awful social skills right along into adulthood. They are brash and blame the very people they abuse for causing their actions. "I couldn't tell you I took the money out of your purse. You would have gotten hysterical. I can't even talk to you." Or (after they have yet again exploited you in any number of ways), "I can never talk to you. You never listen to what I want."

10 Signs That You're in a Relationship with a Narcissist

Narcissism is often interpreted in popular culture as a person who's in love with him or herself. It is more accurate to characterize the pathological narcissist as someone who's in love with an idealized self-image, which they project to avoid feeling (and being seen as) the real, disenfranchised, wounded self. Deep down, most pathological narcissists feel like the "ugly duckling," even if they painfully don't want to admit it.

How do you know when you're dealing with a narcissist? While most of us are guilty of some of the following behaviours at one time or another, a pathological narcissist tends to dwell habitually in several of the following personas, while remaining largely unaware of (or unconcerned with) how his or her actions affect others.

1. Conversation Hoarder. The narcissist loves to talk about him or herself and doesn't give you a chance to take part in a two-way conversation. You struggle to have your views and feelings heard. When you do get a word in, if it's not in agreement with the narcissist, your comments are likely to be corrected, dismissed, or ignored.

"My father's favourite responses to my views were: 'but…,' 'actually…,' and 'there's more to it than this…' He always has to feel like he knows better."— Anonymous

2. Conversation Interrupter. While many people have the poor communication habit of interrupting others, the narcissist interrupts and quickly switches the focus back to herself. He shows little genuine interest in you.

3. Rule Breaker. The narcissist enjoys getting away with violating rules and social norms, such as cutting in line, chronic under-tipping (some will overtip to show off), stealing office supplies, breaking multiple appointments, or disobeying traffic laws.

"I take pride in persuading people to give me exceptions to their rules"— Anonymous

4. Boundary Violator. Shows wanton disregard for other people's thoughts, feelings, possessions, and physical space. Oversteps and uses others without consideration or sensitivity. Borrows items or money without returning. Breaks promises and obligations repeatedly. Shows little remorse and blames the victim for one's lack of respect.

"It's your fault that I forgot because you didn't remind me"— Anonymous

5. False Image Projection. Many narcissists like to do things to impress others by making themselves look good externally. This "trophy" complex can exhibit itself physically, romantically, sexually, socially, religiously, financially, materially, professionally, academically, or culturally. In these situations, the narcissist uses people,

objects, status, and accomplishments to represent the self, substituting for the perceived, inadequate "real" self. These grandstanding "merit badges" are often exaggerated. The underlying message of this type of display is: "I'm better than you!" or "Look at how special I am—I'm worthy of everyone's love, admiration, and acceptance!"

"I dyed my hair blond and enlarged my breasts to get men's attention—and to make other women jealous"— Anonymous

"My accomplishments are everything"— Anonymous executive

"I never want to be looked upon as poor. My fiancé and I each drive a Mercedes. The best man at our upcoming wedding also drives a Mercedes."— Anonymous

In a big way, these external symbols become pivotal parts of the narcissist's false identity, replacing the real and injured self.

6. Entitlement. Narcissists often expect preferential treatment from others. They expect others to cater (often instantly) to their needs, without being considerate in return. In their mindset, the world revolves around them.

7. Charmer. Narcissists can be very charismatic and persuasive. When they're interested in you (for their gratification), they make you feel very special and wanted. However, once they lose interest in you (most likely after they've gotten what they want, or became bored), they may drop you without a second thought. A narcissist can be

very engaging and sociable, as long as you're fulfilling what she desires, and giving her all of your attention.

8. Grandiose Personality. Thinking of oneself as a hero or heroine, a prince or princess, or one of a kind special person. Some narcissists have an exaggerated sense of self-importance, believing that others cannot live or survive without his or her magnificent contributions.

"I'm looking for a man who will treat my daughter and me like princesses"— Anonymous singles ad

"Once again I saved the day—without me, they're nothing"— Anonymous

9. Negative Emotions. Many narcissists enjoy spreading and arousing negative emotions to gain attention, feel powerful, and keep you insecure and off-balance. They are easily upset at any real or perceived slights or inattentiveness. They may throw a tantrum if you disagree with their views, or fail to meet their expectations. They are extremely sensitive to criticism and typically respond with the heated argument (fight) or cold detachment (flight). On the other hand, narcissists are often quick to judge, criticize, ridicule, and blame you. Some narcissists are emotionally abusive. By making you feel inferior, they boost their fragile ego and feel better about themselves.

"Some people try to be tall by cutting off the heads of others"— Paramhansa Yogananda.

10. Manipulation: Using Others as an Extension of Self. Making decisions for others to suit one's own needs. The narcissist may use his or her romantic partner, child, friend, or colleague to meet unreasonable self-serving needs, fulfil unrealized dreams, or cover up self-perceived inadequacies and flaws.

"If my son doesn't grow up to be a professional baseball player, I'll disown him"— Anonymous father

"Aren't you beautiful? Aren't you beautiful? You're going to be just as pretty as mommy" — Anonymous mother

Another way narcissists manipulate is through guilt, such as proclaiming, "I've given you so much, and you're so ungrateful," or, "I'm a victim—you must help me, or you're not a good person." They hijack your emotions and beguile you to make unreasonable sacrifices.

CHAPTER 3

HOW TO PREVENT AND AVIOD NARCISSISTIC ABUSE

The Season of the Narcissistic Emotional Abuser

All things have a season. There was a season before the narcissistic emotional abuser in your life. There was or is a season of the narcissistic emotional abuser in your life. And surely, there is or can be the season after the narcissistic emotional abuser in your life. One season preparing the soil for the next season as is the natural progression of life.

It doesn't occur to you to question, "How on earth did I get into this mess?" before the narcissistic emotional abuser entered your life. No, you were probably asking yourself the question, most likely years before that question, something to the effect of, "Why did he/she/they do this to me?" That question wasn't about the abuse caused by the narcissistic emotional abuser with whom you fell in love as an adult. No, that question quite possibly would have been about the abuse caused by a different type of abuser in your life when you were but a child, many times a sexual abuser.

This is not to say the sexual abuser was not also a narcissist, as sexual abusers exhibit three of the minimum of five criteria needed to be "diagnosable." This is not to say that all those who find themselves having stories to tell of having been involved with a narcissistic emotional abuser have been victims of the trauma caused by childhood sexual abuse. Therein, however, exists the very strong possibility that someone did something to you in the early years of your life that prepared your "soil" to attract and be attracted to a narcissistic emotional abuser.

In the midst of being in the season of the narcissistic emotional abuser, you begin to realize that a change has begun to take place in the way you are thinking and the way you are talking. At the beginning of this season, when talking to those by your side experiencing near to the same emotional pain that you is experiencing due to your repeated return to the abuser, your conversations focused on what they, the narcissistic emotional abuser, was doing or more often not doing. Now, your focus is on you asking yourself, "How did I get in this crazy mess?" You begin to acknowledge your accomplishments and who you are or what you have gained in life. You begin to compare yourself to the others that you know exist in what you want to believe is an exclusive relationship.

In the midst of this season, you begin to do some soul searching. Your question of, "How did I get in this mess?" no longer is just a glib question. This question miraculously begins to take on entire new energy. It wants an answer. It demands an answer. You are the owner of the question, and you hold the key to give you the answer.

The journey of finding your answer, be forewarned, is not an easy or painless journey. Assuredly you will go through life on some sort of another journey if not on the one searching for your answer. You have the choice to run towards or run away from your answer. In the running towards your answer, you have the chance to eventually find peace and healing. In the running away from your answer you take the chance of continuing to experience emotional abuse in your life and yet another.

How to Handle Narcissistic Abuse

We're all capable of abuse when we're frustrated or hurt. We may be guilty of criticizing, judging, withholding, and controlling, but some abusers, including narcissists, take abuse to a different level. Narcissistic Abuse can be physical, mental, emotional, sexual, financial, and spiritual. Some types of emotional abuse are not easy to spot, including manipulation. It can include emotional blackmail, using threats and intimidation to exercise control. Narcissists are masters of verbal abuse and manipulation. They can go so far as to make you doubt your perceptions, called gas lighting.

The Motivation for Narcissistic Abuse

Remember that narcissistic personality disorder (NPD) and abuse exist on a continuum, ranging from silence to violence. Rarely will a narcissist take responsibility for his or her behaviour. Generally, they deny their actions and augment the abuse by blaming the victim. Particularly, malignant narcissists aren't bothered by guilt. They can be sadistic and take pleasure in inflicting pain. They can be so competitive and unprincipled that they engage in anti-social behaviour. Don't confuse narcissism with an anti-social personality disorder.

The objective of narcissistic abuse is power. They act with the intent to diminish or even hurt other people. The most important thing to remember about intentional abuse is that it's designed to dominate you. Abusers' goals are to increase their control and authority while creating doubt, shame, and dependency in their victims. They want to feel superior to avoid hidden feelings of inferiority. Understanding this can empower you. Like all bullies, despite their defences of rage, arrogance, and self-inflation, they suffer from shame. Appearing weak and humiliated is their biggest fear. Knowing this, it's essential not to take personally the words and actions of an abuser. This enables you to confront narcissistic abuse.

Mistakes in Dealing with Abuse

When you forget an abuser's motives, you may naturally react in some of these ineffective ways:

1. Appeasement. If you placate to avoid conflict and anger, it empowers the abuser, who sees it as weakness and an opportunity to exert more control.

2. Pleading. This also shows weakness, which narcissists despise in themselves and others. They may react dismissively with contempt or disgust.

3. Withdrawal. This is a good temporary tactic to collect your thoughts and emotions but it is not an effective strategy to deal with abuse.

4. Arguing and Fighting. Arguing over the facts wastes your energy. Most abusers aren't interested in the facts, but only in justifying their position and being right. Verbal arguments can quickly escalate to fights that drain and damage you. Nothing is gained. You lose and can end up feeling more victimized, hurt, and hopeless.

5. Explaining and Defending. Anything beyond a simple denial of a false accusation leaves you open to more abuse. When you address the content of what is being said and explain and defend your position, you endorse an abuser's right to judge, approve, or abuse you. Your reaction sends this message: "You have power over my self-esteem. You have the right to approve or disapprove of me. You're entitled to be my judge."

6. Seeking Understanding. This can drive your behaviour if you desperately want to be understood. It's based on the false hope that a narcissist is interested in understanding you, while a narcissist is only interested in winning a conflict and having a superior position. Depending upon the degree of narcissism, sharing your feelings may also expose you to more hurt or manipulation. It's better to share your feelings with someone safe who cares about them.

7. Criticizing and Complaining. Although they may act tough, because abusers are insecure, inside they're fragile. They can dish it, but can't take it. Complaining or criticizing an abuser can provoke rage and vindictiveness.

8. Threats. Making threats can lead to retaliation or backfire if you don't carry them out. Never make a threat

you're not ready to enforce. Boundaries with direct consequences are more effective.

9. Denial. Don't fall into the trap of denial by excusing, minimizing, or rationalizing abuse. And don't fantasize that it will go away or improve at some future time. The longer it goes on, the more it grows, and the weaker you can become.

10. Self-Blame Don't blame yourself for an abuser's actions and try harder to be perfect. This is a delusion. You can't cause anyone to abuse you. You're only responsible for your behaviour. You will never be perfect enough for an abuser to stop their behaviour, which stems from their insecurities, not you.

Confronting Abuse Effectively

Allowing abuse damages your self-esteem. Thus, it's important to confront it. That doesn't mean to fight and argue. It means standing your ground and speaking up for yourself clearly and calmly and having boundaries to protect your mind, emotions, and body. Before you set boundaries, you must:

1. Know Your Rights. You must feel entitled to be treated with respect and that you have specific rights, such as the right to your feelings, the right not to have sex if you decline, a right to privacy, a right not to be yelled at, touched, or disrespected. If you've been abused a long time (or as a child), your self- esteem likely has been

diminished. You may no longer trust yourself or have confidence.

2. Be Assertive. This takes learning and practice to avoid being passive or aggressive. Try these short-term responses to dealing with verbal putdowns:

* I'll think about it.

* I'll never be the good enough wife (husband) that you hoped for

* I don't like it when you criticize me. Please stop." (Then walk away)

* That's your opinion. I disagree, (or) I don't see it that way.

* You're saying... " (Repeat what was said. Add, "Oh, I see.")

* I won't talk to you when you (describe abuse, e.g. "belittle me"). Then leave.

* Agree to the part that's true. "Yes, I burned the dinner." Ignore

You're a rotten cook.

* Humor - "You're very cute when you get annoyed.

3. Be Strategic. Know what you want specifically, what the narcissist wants, what your limits are, and where you have power in the relationship. You're dealing with someone

highly defensive with a personality disorder. There are specific strategies to having an impact.

4. Set Boundaries. Boundaries are rules that govern the way you want to be treated. People will treat you the way you allow them to. You must know what your boundaries are before you can communicate them. This means getting in touch with your feelings, listening to your body, knowing your rights, and learning assertiveness. They must be explicit.

Don't hint or expect people to read your mind.

5. Have Consequences. After setting boundaries, if they're ignored, it's important to communicate and invoke consequences. These are not threats, but the actions you take to protect yourself or meet your needs.

6. Be Educative. Research shows that narcissists have neurological deficits that affect their interpersonal reactions. You're the best approach is to educate a narcissist like a child. Explain the impact of their behaviour and provide incentives and encouragement for different behaviour. This may involve communicating consequences. It requires planning what you're going to say without being emotional.

Narcissistic Individuals Target Your Greatest Fears and Weaknesses

Individuals with narcissistic personality disorder are uncannily intuitive. They 'read' people. The narcissistic personality relies on obtaining other people's attention and knows exactly which buttons to push to get 'energy', otherwise known as narcissistic supply - the drug that allows the narcissist to feel significant, and 'alive'.

A narcissistic personality wishes to secure energy and ensure a place to project his or her damaged and tormented self on to. The narcissist is conscienceless, he or she has no remorse in using your weakest links against you.

Because the narcissistic personality operates as a chameleon, he or she may change tactics from person to person and from relationship to relationship, depending on the individual he or she is dealing with.

Within a short amount of time, if the narcissist has decided to secure you as narcissistic supply, he or she will win your confidence by being extremely attentive in getting to know you.

The purpose of this is to build information. The narcissistic personality looks for vulnerabilities, weak links and insecurities, which he or she can play on down the track to confuse and abuse.

It may seem ludicrous that a person hurting you with your insecurities can manipulate you to stay hooked while they abuse you. People with narcissistic personality disorder use gas lighting and projection people with high levels of conscience because they hate to feel like they are 'wrong' and 'misunderstood', this grants the perfect psychological cocktail for the narcissist to operate abominably while his or her victim stays attached trying to prove integrity to the narcissist.

Trying to win clemency, validation and approval from an individual with a narcissistic personality disorder is a deadly game. The narcissistic personality knows where to hit you at your lowest mark, at you most vulnerable, raw and insecure place. This leaves you reeling in disbelief, horror and dismay over how a person who claims to love you, care for you and who regularly gushes adoration at you, could be capable of such an atrocity. All logic regarding looking after self (leaving) may be non-existent in the fighting for decency in the face of such emotional onslaughts and shock.

You may believe the details of what the narcissist attacks you with matter to him or her. The truth is they don't. The narcissistic personality is uninterested in the 'details' of arguments. The narcissist is simply looking for 'reactions' from you.

The narcissistic personality isn't interested in justice, truth or your integrity. The narcissist thrives off your pain and loves the fact that all of his or her inner torment can be projected on to you, and you become the crazy, hurt and deranged one.

The moral to this story is, absolutely get to know people's integrity and character before sharing all your deep, dark secrets. Additionally your approval of self, regardless of other's opinions, safeguards you against having to prove yourself fruitlessly, all the way to your demise, to a person who has no remorse or conscience.

7 Phases of Narcissistic Abuse (and How to Stop It No Matter Where You Are)

Phases of narcissistic abuse

There are stages of abuse used by the narcissistic individual. After all, narcissism is a mental illness, sometimes uncontrollable and debilitating. These stages make it extremely difficult to see the truth behind the behaviour of narcissistic abuse. Here's a secret, however. You can stop this narcissistic abuse during any of these stages.

The honeymoon phase

When you first enter a relationship with a narcissist, you will have no clue who they are. The narcissist will seem like your soul mate, the perfect partner. He will shower you with attention and gifts. He will compliment you on your beauty and personality. If you are a young adult, you will all head over heels for him. If you are an older adult who is unaware of this phase of narcissism, you may also be easily fooled.

The honeymoon phase is so skillfully crafted to fulfil the needs of the narcissist, that it will seem legitimate. For a moment, the narcissist will truly be in love and filling a deep void within. So, it's no wonder why the honeymoon phase can seem like a dream come true.

Solution: Remember, never give too much of yourself during good times. Yes, it is important to let your walls down with someone who truly cares about you, but be careful. There's nothing wrong with protecting your emotions and your mind by limiting how much you choose to give away.

The fading phase

Over time, the interest of the narcissist will fade. You will notice they aren't as attentive as before, and they even stop giving compliments. Soon, the narcissist will become distant, and you will find yourself becoming clingy. After all, you were once spoiled by the lavish treatment you received before, and it's hard to adapt to sudden changes. The closer you get, the more they will pull away.

Solution: Make sure you retain those interests you had before you met someone. Spend time with family and friends so that the fading phase will not damage you as much as it could. This treatment is wrong, but you don't have to become a victim by falling into its trap.

The emotional phase

By this time, emotions are heightened from the push and pull of the changes occurring the narcissistic abuse. The strength of the relationship has faded, and anger and loneliness begin to take its place. The narcissist grows even more distant leaving their mate confused and hurt. During the phase, the narcissist will continue to pull further away as you try harder to mend what's broken.

Solution: Stop! Right now, just stop trying to pull them closer. Let them grow as distant as they please, and they will notice how you aren't chasing them. This will further reveal who they are. I guarantee they will accuse you of being the one who grew distant. This blame game will prove their serious mental illness to be true.

Anger and fighting phase

You may now start to make attempts to mend the relationship by confronting the narcissist. Unfortunately, confrontation never works with this type of personality. Fighting will start, and then the silent treatment will be used to keep you from forcing the narcissist to look at the truth of their behaviour. Before long, this silent treatment will force you to be the one to apologize, leaving you back where you started, with no answers and feeling alone again.

Solution: This will be hard, but no matter how much the narcissist uses the silent treatment, do not give in. You will feel lonely and hurt, but you should remain strong.

Self-blame phase

Now, we are convinced the whole break down of the relationship is our fault. Our self-esteem starts to take a hit, and we become obsessed with trying to fix the problems.

We lose ourselves to the narcissist as we try desperately to make them happy. They have already lost interest, and this effort is ignored. Now we start to think we are crazy and we wonder who the person is that we once loved.

Solution: When you start to blame yourself, make a list. List all the actions and words used by the narcissist. Then you will see that none of this breakdown was ever your doing.

The end game

Whether the narcissist ends the relationship or you do it, it will be a gift. Sometimes the narcissist, although they have lost interest in you, will keep you around for certain satisfaction that you do provide. Some narcissists will get rid of their mates as soon as their interest has faded. It varies from person to person.

If you feel you are being dragged along and there is no hope for release, you will have to end the relationship yourself. This will be difficult because your self-esteem has suffered so much. Sometimes the narcissist has convinced you that no one else would love you. This is a lie and a desperate ploy to keep someone by their side for distraction.

Solution: It's best to leave the relationship unless a serious effort has been done to get help.

The Trap

If you stay, there is a small chance that the narcissist will seek help. If they do not seek help, they will trap you in a cycle of rage and peace. What this means is the narcissist will grow furious about something in which you are to blame for, in their eyes. They will taunt you, call you names and accuse you of being the source of their unhappiness. Since this rage is so intimidating, you will give in and apologize for things that aren't your fault.

The rage will quiet, and the narcissist will go through the cycle of a few weeks of extremely good behaviour. He will compliment you again and spend time with you. This doesn't last, however, and after a few weeks, the rage will return.

Some people in this position find it worth the rage to get the peacetime efforts. This is a trick, a trap, and you should consider getting out of the ordeal for good.

Narcissistic abuse and why it happens

There is no set reason for narcissistic behaviour. Sometimes these traits can be partially genetic. Other times, they come from severe childhood trauma and abuse. Unfortunately, abuse can repeat itself in the form of narcissism because the adult survivor of the abuse has a void which cannot be filled easily by normal behaviour.

If you are dealing with a narcissist, whether it's a family member or a life partner, please seek support. It can be difficult protecting your sanity and health when dealing with an individual of this sort. It's important that you stay healthy and remember your worth.

NARCISSIST

CHAPTER 4

WHY NARCISSISTIC ABUSE SURVIVOR GETS ADDICTED

What Is Narcissistic Abuse?

Narcissists don't love themselves. They're driven by shame. It's the idealized image of themselves, which they convince themselves they embody, that they admire. But deep down, narcissists feel the gap between the façade they show the world and their shame-based self. They work hard to avoid feeling that shame. This gap is true for other codependents, as well, but a narcissist uses defence mechanisms that are destructive to relationships and cause pain and damage to their loved ones' self-esteem.

Many of the narcissist's coping mechanisms are abusive-hence the term, "narcissistic abuse." However, someone can be abusive, but not be a narcissist. Addicts and people with other mental illnesses, such as bipolar disorder and anti-social personality disorder (sociopath) and borderline personality disorders are also abusive, as are many codependents without a mental illness. Abuse is abuse, no matter what is the abuser's diagnosis. If you're a victim of abuse, the main challenges for you are:

- Identifying it;

- Building a support system; and

- Learning how to strengthen and protect yourself.

- What is Narcissistic Abuse

- Abuse may be mental, physical, financial, spiritual, or sexual. Here are a few examples of abuse you may not have identified:

Verbal abuse: Includes belittling, bullying, accusing, blaming, shaming, demanding, ordering, threatening, criticizing, sarcasm, raging, opposing, undermining, interrupting, blocking, and name-calling. Note that many people occasionally make demands, use sarcasm, interrupt, oppose, criticize, blame, or block you. Consider the context, malice, and frequency of the behaviour before labelling it narcissistic abuse.

Manipulation: Generally, manipulation is an indirect influence on someone to behave in a way that furthers the goals of the manipulator. Often, it expresses covert aggression. Think of a "wolf in sheep's clothing." On the surface, the words seem harmless - even complimentary; but underneath you feel demeaned or sense a hostile intent. If you experienced manipulation growing up, you might not recognize it as such.

Emotional blackmail: Emotional blackmail may include threats, anger, warnings, intimidation, or punishment. It's a form of manipulation that provokes doubt in you. You feel a fear, obligation, and or guilt sometimes referred to as "FOG."

Gaslighting: Intentionally making you distrust your perceptions of reality or believe that you're mentally incompetent.

Competition: Competing and one-upping to always be on top, sometimes through unethical means. E.g. cheating in a game.

Negative contrasting: Unnecessarily making comparisons to negatively contrast you with the narcissist or other people.

Sabotage: Disruptive interference with your endeavours or relationships for revenge or personal advantage.

Exploitation and objectification: Using or taking advantage of you for personal ends without regard for your feelings or needs.

Lying: Persistent deception to avoid responsibility or to achieve the narcissist's ends.

Withholding: Withholding such things as money, sex, communication or affection from you.

Neglect: Ignoring the needs of a child for whom the abuser is responsible. Includes child endangerment; i.e., placing or leaving a child in a dangerous situation.

Privacy invasion: Ignoring your boundaries by looking through your things, phone, mail; denying your physical privacy or stalking or following you; ignoring privacy you've requested.

Character assassination or slander: Spreading malicious gossip or lies about you to other people.

Violence: This includes blocking your movement, pulling hair, throwing things, or destroying your property.

Financial abuse: Financial abuse might include controlling you through economic domination or draining your finances through extortion, theft, manipulation, or gambling, or by accruing debt in your name or selling your personal property.

Isolation: Isolating you from friends, family, or access to outside services and support through control, manipulation, verbal abuse, character assassination, or other means of abuse.

Narcissism and the severity of abuse exist on a continuum. It may range from ignoring your feelings to violent aggression. Typically, narcissists don't take responsibility for their behaviour and shift the blame to you or others; however, some do and are capable of feeling guilt and self-reflection.

Malignant Narcissism and Sociopath

Someone with more narcissistic traits who behaves in a malicious, hostile manner is considered to have "malignant narcissism." Malignant narcissists aren't bothered by guilt. They can be sadistic and take pleasure in inflicting pain. They can be so competitive and unprincipled that they engage in anti-social behaviour. Paranoia puts them in a defensive-attack mode as a means of self-protection.

Malignant narcissism can resemble sociopath. Sociopaths have malformed or damaged brains. They display narcissistic traits, but not all narcissists are sociopathic. Their motivations differ. Whereas narcissists prop up an ideal persona to be admired, sociopaths change who they are to achieve their self-serving agenda. They need to win at all costs and think nothing of breaking social norms and laws. They don't attach to people as narcissists do. Narcissists don't want to be abandoned. They're codependent on others' approval, but sociopaths can easily walk away from relationships that don't serve them. Although some narcissists will occasionally plot to obtain their objectives, they're usually more reactive than sociopaths, who coldly calculate their plans.

Get Help

If you're in a relationship with a narcissist, it's important to get outside support to understand clearly what's going on, to rebuild your self-esteem and confidence, and to learn to communicate effectively and set boundaries.

Narcissistic Abuse Survivors Defenseless Against Ignorant Judgment

When people hear that I have chosen to have no contact with my highly toxic, aged mother and father they always tell me how sorry they feel for my parents. I can only assume that in me they see a happy, well-adjusted adult woman and must decide that I have chosen to afflict some sort of maliciously intended punishment on my poor defenceless parents. They cannot possibly understand how violated I feel hearing them defend the very people who nearly destroyed my life; people who would continue to wreak havoc in it if I chose to allow it.

The judgment handed down by the ignorant strikes a raw nerve and immediately put me on the defensive. Cases of appalling abusive actions from my supposedly old, frail, innocent parents, some old some new, come spewing out of my mouth one after another in an attempt to justify my position. My breath is wasted. My stance is never validated. I always end up looking cold-blooded and hard-hearted when in truth I am anything but.

I am a strong, confident woman. I have learned to love myself despite all I have been through. Perhaps it is that air of confidence that causes some to side against me. It must be because everything I stand for in my life demonstrates my compassionate, loving nature, yet all of that seemingly goes right out the window in the eyes of people who do not understand Narcissistic Personality Disorder abuse.

I know that I am not alone in this experience. Due to the covert nature of narcissistic abuse, it is one of the perpetual tragedies many survivors of NPD parents endure. The victim is often seen as the perpetrator and the perpetrator seen as the victim. Even when we find the courage to stop the abuse we can never redeem ourselves in the minds of the judgmental ignoramus, professional or otherwise.

As NPD abuse survivors our healing must come entirely from our courageous resolve. The Narcissistic Personality Disorder parent will never validate our feelings, verify our memories, or allow us our pain. Our friends, co-workers and acquaintances who cannot possibly understand what we go through often say the wrong thing, making us feel even worse. The only possibility of support is an alliance with siblings who have shared our experiences and have likewise abandoned their denial.

I am very fortunate. It took a few years, but my sisters both embraced the truth. We can emotionally support each other and have formed an ironclad alliance against our toxic parents, but that is uncommon. More often than not, siblings side with parents who are adept at exploiting their victimization and rallying sympathizers around them, alienating their recovering brother or sister even further.

NPD survivors must have a solid support system to keep them from self-destruction. Rationality does not exist in dealings with those who have Narcissistic Personality Disorder. Rational minds cannot make sense of NPD irrational behaviour, though that does not stop us from trying to rationalize the confusion we experience. It is that effort that makes us feel as if we are the crazy ones.

It takes a great deal of validation to convince us that we are not crazy. That is why I strongly recommend survivors work with a professional therapist, psychologist or counsellor who is highly skilled in working with Narcissistic Personality Disorder abuse until they feel strong and confident enough to stand on their own-however long that takes. That is the formula for success in completely overcoming the pain-for confidently moving forward in our lives.

There will always be issues throughout our lives that challenge us as NPD abuse survivors. Though I counsel other survivors and extensively write, speak and am highly knowledgeable about Narcissistic Personality Disorder, I am not immune to its ugly assaults. However, as a result of the work, I have done I am confident and skilled enough to get through them. The more healing work we do, the stronger we get and the easier those challenges are to deal with.

You have survived one of the most insidious forms of child abuse. Though often invisible, the abuse was real; your pain is real. But never choose to be a victim of your past. Reclaim your power. Start today.

7 Signs You've Arrived as a Survivor of Narcissistic Abuse

Recovering from narcissistic and emotional abuse can seem like an ordeal of the most grievous kind.

You may have endured months of struggle and suffering without knowing if you're making any progress because the pull to go back remains strong. You miss the moments under your abuser's sway because, in your traumatized mind, cognitive dissonance and memories of so-called "good times" cloud your objectivity.

How do you know where you stand on your road to recovery? Victory isn't always in-your-face. Arriving as a survivor of narcissistic abuse comes in waves, even ripples, but if you experience the following seven signs, you can feel gratified knowing that healing is within your reach.

1) You've begun to appreciate that self-care is something you need to participate in consistently.

Not only because you are healing from emotional abuse, but because healthy people, in general, understand the importance of putting on their oxygen mask before they can help others.

Life can be stressful enough without the added obstacle of toxic abuse. It only stands to reason that if you're healing from narcissistic abuse, your body and mind require extreme self-care. This might include reducing social engagements, staying off of the internet, saying "no" to friends and family, taking a nap when you feel exhausted, and making time to do meditations.

You resist the urge to make excuses as to why you can't take care of yourself, realizing that even single mothers can work self-care into their schedules. If you are a single mother, you deliberately get a babysitter on occasion to take yourself out. You do guide meditations at night. Your journal and do mirror work. If a friend asks you to visit and you don't have the energy, you respectfully decline. You take the initiative to be a little "selfish" because you understand the need to do so after putting out other people's fires for too long.

2) You do what it takes to protect your mental and physical space.

You no longer acquiesce to things that intrude on your privacy and peace of mind.

Most narcissists and other Cluster-B disordered individuals pull out all the stops when trying to hook a previous source of supply back into their realm of crazy. They pretend to have changed, to want to be friends (especially for the "sake of the kids"), to be just another normal person going through a typical breakup or divorce. They may go so far as to tell you their relationship problems with their new partner.

Arriving as a survivor means you no longer want, nor tolerate, any of those things. You want peace and autonomy so badly that you are willing to go complete No Contact and resolve not to let them into your home anymore. You don't leave yourself open to any of their tomfoolery, and instead, put up all necessary boundaries to protect your new sense of peace.

3) You no longer care about how your Ex will react to your decisions.

You don't worry whether your life choices will make your Ex angry or make life "inconvenient" for them. You understand that true fulfilment means honouring your dreams, desires, and ambitions regardless of how your ex may respond. As long as you abide by any court orders in place, you know that your future is in your own hands.

4) You may start to notice that some of your other relationships have been a big energy and time drain, and you resolve to do something about them.

You've gotten into the habit of honouring yourself and releasing that which doesn't serve your highest good. Consequently, you've become more sensitive to other relationships in which you feel taken advantage of. This doesn't mean that you would dump a friend in need, but rather that you've started noticing your relationship 'climates'. In the same way that a long-term weather pattern creates a climate in a particular region, if the climate of any of your relationships has proven – over time – that you typically feel put upon and used, then those are the ones that you now consider releasing.

5) You're more concerned about what you're doing with your life than what your Ex is doing with theirs.

You no longer obsess about your Ex with their new supply or the fact that they seem so happy because you've come to understand that your Ex is destined to repeat the same cycle of abuse with anyone they are with at any given time.

6) You no longer focus on problems, but on solutions.

You realize that you have the power to conquer and change your circumstances, rather than remain defenceless against whatever stunts your Ex might be playing.

You understand that for every action, there is an equal and opposite reaction. If you need to delete an email you've had for years because your Ex emails you from different accounts, you delete it. If you need to file a restraining order because your Ex is stalking and harassing you, you drive to the courthouse and file it. If you see the need to change your cell phone number and insist that they call you on your landline, you do so. If your Ex sends you unwanted gifts and flowers, you mark them "return to sender" or refuse the delivery. You fight the good fight to protect your newfound freedom.

7) You no longer consider what happened to you a punishment, but rather an eye-opener because you understand that it happened so you could heal the wounds you've carried since childhood.

You've arrived as a survivor from narcissistic abuse because you no longer look to your Ex for approval or appreciation, knowing that even the appearance of those things comes with a high price. You accept that there are people whose behaviour is disturbingly damaging, but you no longer open yourself up to it. Instead, you respond appropriately, with full awareness of why it's necessary to do so.

You've arrived as a survivor because you no longer tolerate anything that discounts your value – from anyone – for you've become your own best friend and advocate.

Forgive or Not Forgive Narcissistic Abuser?

Should Narcissistic Abusers Be Held Accountable for Their Actions?

Many recovering victims of narcissistic abuse struggle with the dilemma of whether or not to hold the narcissist accountable for his behaviour. We learn in our recovery that narcissism is a personality disorder and wonder, "Isn't having a personality disorder the same thing as having a mental illness? And if so, how can we hold a mentally ill person responsible for their actions?"

One reason we find ourselves in this conundrum is that for many years we have been trained by the narcissist to first sacrifice our own needs for theirs. So it stands to reason, given our brainwashing and our typically gentle forgiving natures that we overlook our suffering and wonder if narcissists are to be pitied for their lack of self-control.

And where does forgiveness fit in? Can and should we forgive them for their actions if we believe they cannot control them? What if we believe that they can control their behaviour but find it difficult to do so? And should we forgive them if we believe that they are in complete control of their behaviours?

There are two schools of thought on the culpability of the narcissist. I'll first talk about the less popular of the two.

Some say that the narcissist does what he does without conscious regard; that he does not premeditate his campaign of abuse. And when he is functioning on a conscious level, he is unable to predict the outcomes of his actions or control his behaviour.

This theory may be true in part but is not substantiated as a whole, though both theories do agree that the narcissist lacks impulse control. And they both maintain that because he lacks impulse control, he is not entirely responsible for his actions.

That is where the schools of thought differ. One believes that he is entirely at the mercy of his disorder; the other believes that he is partially at the mercy of it.

The second school of thought is that the decisions that propel the narcissist into action are unconsciously experienced, but that the narcissist is in complete control of how and when he will act them out. This theory maintains that he knows what is right and what is wrong, that he can anticipate the results of his actions, and that he is fully aware of the penalty others will pay for his choices. So the decision of whether or not to act on his compulsions is made consciously and calculatingly.

The problem for the narcissist is that suppressing his compulsions is not an option he is willing to take. And why should he? He doesn't care about anyone but himself.

As far as the narcissist is concerned, people only exist as sources of his narcissistic supply; sources of adoration, admiration, and attention. One person doesn't mean any more to him than another does. People are dispensable and interchangeable; they are merely a means to an end. So if one person doesn't give him what he wants, he disposes of them like trash and moves onto another source of supply.

The narcissist satisfies his never-ending hunger for attention at the expense of anyone naïve enough, dependent enough, or willing enough to feed him. He is an addict who will stoop to any level to get his fix. Since he cannot empathize, he does not have to experience the implications of what he does to others. He may know that you are hurting, but he can't feel your pain.

Narcissists are consumed by inner turmoil, conflict and fear. And what do they fear the most? They fear to lose their narcissistic supply; the supply they get from us. Acting out on their compulsions like parasites is how they alleviate the pressure and anxiety that restlessly stirs inside them. And they don't have a conscience regarding their treatment of others. They don't care about or feel responsible for whoever must be sacrificed or expended to fulfil their needs.

Narcissists may lack empathy, but they do not lack emotion. They are highly sensitive, though they only experience that sensitivity as it relates to them. And they do not experience emotion the way other people do. They have a false self; a powerful defence mechanism that keeps them from having to deeply feel their emotions. It keeps them from feeling responsible for anything that goes on in their lives.

They do feel pity, but only as it relates to their self and their interests. Because they have a false sense of grandiosity, they feel forever victimized. They see life as being unfair to them; they feel like they never get all they deserve. They believe that everyone owes them all the time.

But should we feel sorry for someone who is ruled by their fears and suffers a great deal emotionally? The answer is no... we should not. Who among us does not have emotional pain and feel fear? And haven't we suffered a great deal of pain and fear at the hands of the narcissist? We are the casualties of their behaviour; not the other way around.

The degree to which any human being suffers is directly related to how much he allows these common human emotions to impact his everyday life. The narcissist cowers and victimizes others in the face of his pain and fear. We do not. We draw on our inner strength and courage in the face of our pain and fear.

So narcissists have a personality disorder, but are they mentally ill innocents who know not what they do? Think about it this way. How many times have you witnessed the two faces of your narcissist? How many times have you seen him behave entirely different, with different people, under the same circumstances? How many times have you seen him control his behaviour when others are there to witness it, and then completely go off on you when no one is there to see it happen? The fact that he only acts out only when he thinks he can get away with it demonstrates the existence of choice.

And how many times have you seen your narcissist pouring on the charm with someone they think is important, influential, famous, or wealthy? These people are the narcissist's ideal. It doesn't matter what the person's morals or ethics are. Their position in life is the only thing that attracts the narcissist who believes that because he is unique and special, he should only engage with other special, rich, or accomplished people. Narcissists are attracted to wealthy people, beautiful people, and successful people who they believe they can benefit from in some way or which will enhance their self-image by association.

The fact that narcissists can turn their charm on and off, just as they would a light switch, is further evidence demonstrating the existence of choice and while the narcissist can admire these people, he is also envious of them and what they have that he does not. That is because narcissists live in a state of constant envy.

Narcissists are envious of everyone. They envy the fact that others have feelings. They envy others' houses, education, marriages, children, station in life, careers. They especially envy the fact that others are happy.

Being around happy people exaggerates their sense of deprivation and their misery. Happiness in others provokes viciousness in narcissists. They will do almost anything to snuff the light out of someone who is happy, especially someone who they feel they have control over. If they can't safely lash out at their target, they will lie and badmouth them to others, or do a slow burn about it and then blame or take it out on someone close to them. Making themselves feel better by making other people feel worse, reinforces their sense of omnipotence. They make it clear that those close to them are only allowed to feel happy when they want them to.

Narcissists do not feel remorse for the abuse they inflict on those closest to them. The narcissist sees them as easy marks that he does not have to try to win over; extensions of himself. He just takes it for granted that they are there for him, safely and readily at his disposal, to abuse as he pleases and fulfils his narcissistic supply as needed.

Have you ever told your narcissist that he is hurting your feelings or expressed how badly he is making you feel? Have you ever asked him to stop treating you the way he does?

Anyone who loves and cares about you would take your feelings into consideration, but not so for the narcissist. He sees your vulnerability the same way a lion sees a young gazelle. It provokes his predatory urges even more.

It also adds fuel to his fire. He is appalled that you would question his actions. Any suggestion that you see anything he does as less than perfect enrages him if you have lived with a narcissist you understand how terrifying being the target of narcissistic rage can be.

Narcissistic rage is a defence mechanism the narcissist's false self employs to protect his fragile ego.

But it is also a control mechanism meant to erode your self-confidence, intimidate you, humiliate you, and disable you; all to keep you around so he can continue to feed off of you.

Though the rage may be difficult for someone with a narcissistic personality disorder to control, the motive used to keep you in line is deliberate. They are fully aware of what they are doing but simply do not care.

CHAPTER 5

TIPS FOR COPING IN RELATIONSHIP WITH NARCISSISTS

Are You in a Relationship With a Narcissist?

If you are in a relationship with a narcissist you're living in hell on earth. A narcissist is someone who constantly belittles you at the drop of a hat. A narcissist makes you feel like a peasant while he is the king of not only his domain but yours. You spend every waking moment catering to their every wish, while all your wishes never come true. A narcissist doesn't care about your wishes, hopes, dreams, feelings, judgment or needs. A narcissist only cares about their own, and so should you, or you will be sorry.

You may try to keep the peace, but with a narcissist, peace is impossible. They create standards you can never reach so that you will fail again and again, and it is up to them to dish out your punishment. And dish it out they will. Since you are all alone with your thoughts and feelings and are unable to verbalize them or exhibit them, you will feel like a robot, and a very lonely robot to boot. How did someone so promising and charming hide the fact that they are a narcissist? How did you not see this coming?

A narcissist is always different at the beginning of a relationship, way different. They come across as prince charming, sweep you off your feet and place you on this pedestal and treat you in a way you thought only happened in fairy tales. Once you have fallen under their spell, a narcissist then lets his facade crumble. Not to the outside world though. Just in your personal life. They maintain their image for all the world to see but allow you to see what is behind the mask, and it is what nightmares are made of.

A relationship with a narcissist is a one-way street. The street leads towards them, and away from you. When you are in a relationship with a narcissist, you must constantly cater to them and build and maintain their inflated ego and sense of self at the expense of your self-esteem, dignity, and ego. Compassion will rarely be given to you by a narcissist, but they expect and demand it from you.

The term "double standards" is perfect to describe a relationship with a narcissist. It is all about them and has nothing to do with you. They get the praise; you get the complains and reprimands. They have a say on everything, you are afraid to say anything and better keep your mouth shut. If they are not happy, you will not be allowed to be happy either. A narcissist doesn't care about your happiness; they are only concerned with their own.

Since narcissists are so in love with themselves, they cannot be capable of really loving you because they can never put you first. Sure, if you try and end things with a narcissist, they may go overboard to get you back. But is it really because they love you and will change? No, it is for their ego, they do not want to be abandoned. THEY can leave YOU, but you cannot leave THEM. So how do you know if you are involved with a narcissist as a friend, lover or family tie?

A narcissist has an over-inflated ego and thinks they are above others and look down on everyone else they deem not up to their standards. Because they are special, rules do not apply to them. To everyone else, yes, but to them, no. A narcissist has delusions of grandeur. They are not ordinary so why should they have an ordinary wife, ordinary kids and ordinary job or an ordinary house? That may be good enough for "other people" but not for them. They have a sense of entitlement like no one you have ever met before or since. They think other people are jealous of them or out to get them.

Narcissists feel you should be able to take criticism from them, and they will give it to you constantly. However, you cannot criticize them for ANYTHING. They will also twist your words and take things you said critically when you did not mean it that way. They will have temper tantrums when they are unhappy over any little thing.

Narcissists will keep you guessing. One day they act like all is wonderful and they adore you, the next day, they are as cold as ice and treat you like a stranger or an enemy. A narcissist cannot sympathize or empathize with anyone other than themselves. Other people's feelings, unless it is to get what something from them, are irrelevant.

What Makes You Vulnerable to a Narcissistic Partner

There is no "type" that a Narcissistic individual will look to partner up with. They might perceive you as someone who will make them look good, or feel good. If you respond to them in a certain way consistently to feed their need for Narcissistic supply, then this behaviour will draw them to you.

There are traits in you that you can self-examine to see if you have vulnerabilities that attract Narcissistic individuals to you.

1. Not knowing what to look for. A Narcissistic individual will usually look for those who see the very best in them. They will usually know how to be so "in tuned" with you. It doesn't mean that they are. If you are left thinking, this is too good to be true. They shower with you with love and attention. They seemed to almost "read your mind," especially in the beginning stages. This is, so you fall in love with them. When you don't recognize the early stages behaviour that a Narcissistic person displays, you will fall right into their hands. Better for you to get familiar with what those signs are, and slow things down from the beginning. Someone can only mask their behaviour for so long before their true colours show.

2. You carry the burden for false responsibility in your family of origin. If you have never dealt with those issues that have hindered you from your family of origin, this is where you might fall vulnerable to someone with Narcissistic tendencies. A Narcissistic individual is happy

to have you carry the burdens of your family, as well as their issues while not caring about what you've been through. It's better for you to confront and deal with issues you've been through, so you are not blindsided by being saddled with someone else's issues placed on you. You can't fix another person, nor can they fix you. You can choose to deal with your issues, so they don't continue to be problems that hinder your future relationships. You can also spot someone quicker who wants you to carry the responsibility for their issues, and avoid a toxic relationship much better when you deal with your issues first.

3. You are highly empathic. There's nothing wrong with being empathic. It's a wonderful skill you've developed. It's just when it's one-sided, then it is a problem. If you start noticing, you are always needed to listen when some sort of traumatic drama goes on, but when you need someone to listen to you, the other person is nowhere to be found. If this is an ongoing pattern, beware. Chances are it will stay this way if you say nothing or accept that this is okay. You will find yourself in a one-sided relationship. It's also a sign you might be involved with someone with Narcissistic tendencies. Don't ignore those warning signs that something isn't right. Address it early on.

4. You don't express, or you choose to repress a lot of your own needs. It could be that you might be telling yourself that they need you so that you won't express a whole lot of your own needs. Like number 3, don't ignore this. If you try to rationalize that it's okay for now, it may be that you need to do some personal growth work. No healthy relationship is one-sided. Everyone does have needs from time to time. You might need someone to listen to you when you are

stressed out or to go through a tough time. If you can't talk to that other person, it's time to visit why not.

5. It doesn't feel like a partnership; they want you to re-parent them. We all know someone or seen someone who's "let down their guard," only to find them acting out childishly. You might hear them say, 'you remind me of my mother or my father.' This isn't a good sign. It's likely that person is telling you that they have unhealed wounding from their mother and father and they want to re-create that parent-child relationship again to rework through their unresolved pain. It's not healthy to be in a parent-child relationship where you are the "re-created parent." You'll have an adult child on your hands, not a peer-to-peer relationship. This is also someone who's not ready to be in a relationship with you.

Realize that when you choose to continue a relationship with a Narcissistic individual once you recognize all the symptoms, you will be left with very little in return. You will likely be struggling with frustration, feel like it's a one-sided relationship, and feel incredibly drained from it.

If you're looking for a relationship who will be a real partner to you, then don't choose to be in a relationship with a Narcissist. These individuals, unfortunately, won't be able to meet you in a healthy partnership. It's the early stages of dating where they turn on the charm the most. It's good to know the signs early enough and be aware of what makes you vulnerable to stop before you get too emotionally invested.

How to Deal with a Narcissistic Partner

Some narcissists are obnoxious, offensive and obstinate. Others, however, present as attractive, appealing, easy-going people. It's not until a confrontation occurs that their narcissism becomes obvious.

Summon up the courage to tell him (or her) that he's self-centered and he'll either continue doing whatever he was doing as if you hadn't said anything at all or he will become irate. "Me? Me? Self-centred? How do you think that makes ME feel?" Though all narcissists are not cut from the same cloth, they do have many traits in common. Here are the most typical ones:

1. Narcissists find it hard (if not impossible) to truly appreciate the validity of another's point of view. They imagine that others think and feel the same way they do. If they don't, something's wrong with them.

2. Narcissists need constant validation from the outside. Admire and respect them, and they do fine. Find fault with them and watch out! Grandiose narcissists will strike back venomously; closet narcissists will shrink back into their cave.

3. Narcissists often display a façade self-based on impressive and admirable traits. What's wrong with that? Nothing, if it weren't mere window dressing. Their façade self is fake, covering up a real self that's insecure and vulnerable.

4. Narcissists view others as extensions of themselves. The narcissist sets the standards of behaviour and does not tolerate opposition - especially if your viewpoint requires him to respond in ways he doesn't wish to.

5. Narcissists believe that they are entitled to special treatment. Whether it's a "stupid" law or a "dumb" demand, narcissists feel that they shouldn't have to go along with the pack and confirm. They believe they are of higher status; therefore why to adapt just to please someone else.

6. Narcissists use the money to help them feel special. Status items such as expensive clothes, cars, homes, dinners and trips are essential ways that a narcissist enhances his ego. Spending money, if you have it, is one thing; spending money, if you don't have it, is another. Regardless, a narcissist believes that he deserves the best. And easily fools himself into believing that the money will be there in the future, even if it's not there right now.

7. Narcissists may make a show of being generous by being big tippers or taking care of bills. Look closely, however, and you'll see that their generosity is based upon establishing a reputation for themselves as a VIP.

If you discover that you are living with a narcissist, what can you do to make your life easier?

It may seem weird to say "discover" that you're living with a narcissist, but it's true. Many people don't realize that their partner (or parent or adult child) is a narcissist, discovering it only after much time has elapsed. Why isn't it obvious at the very beginning?

Two reasons:

1. Narcissists are great masters of disguise, describing their behaviour in the best of terms, (i.e. I'm only doing it for you!) Hence, it may take a while for you to 'get' what's going on.

2. Though narcissism has a bad rep (egocentric, egotistical), narcissists also have positive traits. Indeed, they may be quite charismatic and charming. Hence, it may be hard to believe that narcissism is driving their behaviour.

Once you recognize that you are living with a narcissist, here are seven valuable tips for you to maintain your sanity and self-esteem.

1. Know What You Will Tolerate and What You Won't

Trust your judgment. If he (or she) is spending recklessly, know what you will tolerate and what you won't. That doesn't mean that all spending has to be done your way (unless you're two narcissists battling it out). But it does mean that you don't tolerate the narcissist's explanation for free-spending (i.e. Hey, you only live once.") And you take necessary steps (whether he likes it or not) to protect your financial future.

2. Bolster Your Self-Esteem

Do not expect your narcissist to build up your self-esteem when he has just helped tear it down. That is something you must do for yourself. Spend more time with people who think well of you. Get involved with pleasurable activities that bolster your ego. Be kind to yourself.

3. Know when You're being 'Gaslighted'.

When your narcissist says something, then later denies saying it or claims to have said something different, you can begin to doubt your sanity. Were you listening? Were you dreaming? Is she nuts? Am I nuts? What's going on here? Your narcissist may be doing this maliciously to throw you off balance. Or, she may simply be responding to her need of the moment, forgetting what she previously said.

4. Develop a Positive Support System

It may be hard, to be honest with others. You may feel embarrassed, especially if you've been covering for your narcissist for so long. Nevertheless, see if there's a trustworthy friend or family member with whom you can share what's going on. Also, consider seeking the help of a professional who will be able to offer you objective feedback.

5. Don't Tolerate Denigrating Emotional Outbursts

At times you will be upset with each other and need to let off steam. But "how" one lets off steam is vital. If you're being spoken to with disdain and disrespect, stop the action. Make the issue, HOW you are being treated. Express your disappointment. Demand an apology. And if necessary, walk away, letting it be known that you'll be happy to pick up where you left off when you're treated with respect.

6. Learn the Skills of Negotiation

Just because your narcissist wants something, doesn't mean she needs to get it. Just because she expresses herself forcefully, doesn't mean you fold. Everything is negotiable. You just need to know where your power lies. Then you need to convey it and enforce it. The skills of negotiation will empower you in many areas of life - today and in your future.

7. Accept that you are not going to do a total makeover of your narcissist's personality.

Nor should you want to. If your relationship is that bad, consider splitting. But, if there are redeeming traits, see if you can work together to create "family rules" of acceptable behaviour.

Living with a narcissist is not easy. But putting into practice these seven rules will make things more manageable for you.

Relationship Tips - How to Manage Love with a Narcissistic Individual

I am sure you think as overrated the cliche that 'love is blind' - but neuroscience, this prodigy child of science, unveils with an almost cruel satisfaction that some areas of our brains shut down when love comes upon us, blinding the ration from the smart choices we should make.

Brain scans of the people who were madly in love are very similar to the scans of the brains of people who were doing cocaine. There you have it - love is pretty much a drug itself. In a way, we are all drug dealers - the drug of choice being love and other emotional enhancers.

Love could be a wonderful happening if sometimes we wouldn't fall in love with the wrong person. If that person is a narcissist, your burden will reach heights worth of better causes. Either way, you need to learn how to cope with this situation.

According to the American Psychological Association, people with a narcissistic personality disorder display a chronic and pervasive pattern of grandiosity, need for admiration, and lack of empathy.

Narcissists have a grandiose sense of self-importance like they would have a special mission on this earth and they often have a 'king style' type of personality, while all the others should behave as humble servants of their wishes.

They always exaggerate their achievements and talents making everything in their power to gain everybody's attention and recognition. Most of the times they are arrogant and self-absorbed to fulfil their special destiny.

The narcissist will indulge in fantasies of tremendous power, success or beauty, being addicted to the attention and admiration that others manifest. You will find much snobbery between them which they do not deny it but rather be proud of it.

They see themselves as unique masterpieces - God himself obtained his PhD by creating them. Complicated rather than complex personalities, they will find it difficult to empathize with other people.

They can't go out of the perimeter of their personality, not understanding how people don't think the same as they do. That's why many times you may have the feeling of talking to a wall because no matter how deep you explain your point of view, most likely a narcissist will not understand it. A brick and iron wall.

They can't maintain too long relationships, most of the times because people around them give up on explaining themselves over and over again. Narcissist transform their partners in beggars - you will beg for understanding and some unconditional attention and most of the time you will celebrate only leftovers from the feast the narcissist indulged.

You will find many successful individuals with this syndrome because narcissism will drive them to achieve success and accumulate power to feed their self-admiration. Many success achievers has a dose of healthy narcissism - or self-confidence, but healthy narcissism or selfishness will not ask the world to reflect them their inflated self-image and ego.

A relationship with a narcissistic personality will require lots of energy and work because they are in constant need for outside support and approval. Once these needs are fulfilled, they feel powerful, but many times this need will be very hard to be satisfied. They are left feeling vulnerable and lonely - that's how they will explain their "cheating" behaviour.

The genesis of this personality disorder goes back in time to childhood. Most of the time they will be the single child in a family but even then they have been ignored, or the parents had very big expectations of perfection from the child.

The child will fiercely embark on this quest of winning the appreciation of his parents, leaving him with the incapacity to understand other people's needs, as his needs were not understood as a child.

How to detect a narcissist?

1. Be aware of people who advertise themselves too much. They will always want to be in the centre of attention. Being in search of constant approval and admiration they will take over "the stage" and monopolize the discussion and action. They want to be the star in everyone's movie.

2. Lacking empathy toward other people needs. They can't give attention to other people because they are in constant need for that attention. Everyone is a slave and object to fulfil their demands. Narcissist wants all the love, all the attention, all the possessions for themselves - they will be

jealous of other people's achievements and will find it hard to acknowledge their success.

3. They cannot take criticism - it appeals to their childhood memories, and they will reject it with all their power. If you commit the leze-majesty to criticize them, besides the fact that they will deny it, they will feel hurt and unloved. They will never accept responsibility for any wrongdoing and will be on a constant search for finding people to blame for their mistakes.

4. Many will be workaholics - being driven by the huge desire for achievement; they will put all their efforts toward achieving massive success.

It takes time to identify all these character treats as many are under the camouflage of good looking, highly successful people which will always be fascinating and attractive. They can be interesting personalities but very difficult to handle, almost impossible.

The bad news is that they cannot be changed. Read again: narcissist cannot be changed! Since they reject any form of criticism, even the constructive one, they cannot comprehend any wrongdoing and indulge in their self-proclaimed image of perfection. Many of them will have secret thoughts of being god-like and will be blind to any mistake they will do.

It is not recommended to give in to all their demands - you will only just reinforce their grandiose needs, and they will get the feeling that it is normal to have all their wishes fulfilled without them giving much in return.

How to cope with narcissistic partners?

Since they cannot be changed, you need to reevaluate your needs and long term goals for a relationship - it may be interesting for a while to be around such type of people but in the long run it gets exhausting, and anger and resentment will overshadow any feelings of love and tenderness.

1. Do not give in to their never stopping demands, keep your independence from this type of person - if, in any way you depend on them, they will blackmail you to make you give in to their desires.

2. Don't let yourself be infuriated by their lack of empathy or understanding - they are not capable of it. Showing them their incapacity will do nothing - they will blame you for everything that it doesn't work.

3. Finally, decide when enough is enough. A relationship with a narcissist can take you places where you do not want to be, can make you behave in ways you do not recognize yourself. It can undermine your self-esteem and will rob you of the attention you need to give to yourself trying to meet all their needs.

Many artistic personalities will be narcissistic and self-absorbed, ego-centred. The fascination with them will make many of you fall for them since their love will be just like their personality: irrational, instinctual, possessive and overwhelming. Which sometimes will unlock that crazy passionate behaviour within you - fun for a while but it will wear you down and leave you with nothing in the end.

Narcissists will be attached to those that satisfy their needs but will never treat them as partners but as followers. They need to lead and be in control constantly - they do not need equals but disciples or pleasers. The worst thing that can happen is when one narcissist meets someone with low self-esteem - it will be the perfect victim and toy for them.

Stand up for yourself, do not give up on your needs and do not believe all their explanations - their constant need for admiration and approval will make them flirt with many from the opposite sex and not rarely even cheat to reaffirm their power of seduction.

Although they have a certain charisma and aura - probably the outrageous feeling of self-confidence will be their most magnetic treat, they come with a lot of work. Enjoy for as long as you feel that what keeps you together is more than what pushes you apart, but know when to leave as for the moment no treatment is available - besides brain surgery. Guess not, since they consider themselves so perfect.

Let them create if they are artists or achieve the success they want, while you move on and fulfil your emotional and human needs. Love stories can be beautiful without drama and self-proclaimed kings and gods around you.

How to Stop Obsessing Over a Narcissistic Relationship

Obsessing over a narcissistic relationship is stressful and tiring; leading you to feel down, frustrated or hopeless.

Fixating over your painful experience can interfere with your life by keeping you from doing the things you want to do. A particularly helpful skill to stop compulsive thoughts of the abuse is learning to control your attention, the degree to which you are focused on the mistreatment, the more you are aware of it. This is not about denying your pain; it is attending to something else. Negative thoughts are ideas that we tell ourselves and are not always accurate reflections of reality.

When we take feelings too seriously, we let how we feel control all our decisions. While learning to focus on the things you have control over, you will empower yourself to end the destructive attachment. Letting go of your resentments (desire to hurt your partner) happens when you believe in your right to happiness. Sometimes we need time to ready ourselves to cope. Change your thinking about the abuse, and about yourself, so that you don't blame yourself, or believe things are hopeless. The following steps are ways to stop your obsessions.

I believe the first step below requires us to give up our desire for vengeance and letting go of a victim mentality. If you want revenge to let it be your success at creating a decent manageable life. Allowing your abuser to rent space in your head means they get to continue punishing you. Narcissists feel all-powerful when they think your life is miserable with them, and especially without them. Feel your anger and use your emotional pain to motivate change in your life.

Take responsibility for having chosen your abusive partner. Accept the lesson and learn from the relationship pain, so you don't repeat it. Ask yourself, "what is the gift" from this relationship?

Stop talking about your ex-partner to others; refuse to establish a victim identity. Create a state of well-being within you.

Spend time each morning focused on forgiving the narcissist for not being able to love you, so you can free your ego from the desire to hurt them. Move on to a new freedom.

Care enough about your well-being to stop the self-punishing thoughts. Refuse to build drama stories in your mind.

Practice hearing and feeling the critical voice in your head. Banish fear and guilt from your mind. Acknowledge and observe the destructiveness of your compulsive thoughts and emotions.

Keep your thinking and feeling centred on good things, care about how you feel. Lower your dark curtain and emerge from the darkness.

Work as hard on accepting what is good in your life as you have the painful and the difficult. Learn to trust yourself by finding out what is right for you.

4 Relationship Tips to Help You Deal with Your Narcissistic Partner

Jennifer cannot believe how self-absorbed her boyfriend, Sam, is.

She used to be inspired by his confidence, but now it comes off as arrogance. Sam seems more than willing to talk about his life, his day at work and his accomplishments and dreams and unwilling to focus any attention on her.

Sometimes, Jennifer feels like Sam continues to date her just so that he has someone to talk about himself with.

Recently, she became aware of just how narcissistic Sam is when her grandmother-- whom she dearly loves-- died. This was a big deal for Jennifer, and she is still feeling a lot of sadness and grief. Other than a, "So sorry to hear the news" from Sam, Jennifer has received little to no support or comfort from him.

This makes her feel even more empty and sad.

Are you in a love relationship or marriage with someone who seems all caught up in him or herself ? Maybe your partner comes off as arrogant and self-centred. Perhaps your mate can't seem to think or talk about anyone but himself or herself.

If so, you might wonder if your partner is narcissistic.

Being with a narcissistic partner can be painful. You might feel ignored, deficient in some way, irritated, angry and possibly even worried about this apparent personality flaw. You may wonder if your partner needs professional help.

It's true. There is an actual psychological condition called narcissism. It is defined as: "A pattern of traits and behaviours which signify infatuation and obsession with one's self to the exclusion of all others and the egotistic and ruthless pursuit of one's gratification, dominance and ambition."

However, people who appear to be narcissistic may have something else going on. They might not be narcissistic. There is often more to a relationship dynamic than what it appears. For example, your insecurities or fears may cause you to perceive your partner as more self-centred than he or she is.

This doesn't mean that you are wrong and your partner is right or that you don't have valid reasons for how you feel. Not!

What it does mean is that if you want to stay in this relationship and you'd like to experience some improvement around this issue, you're most likely going to need to re-evaluate the situation-- including your role in it.

If you're with a self-absorbed partner, remember these four relationship tips...

#1: Question the labels you're applying.

In the moment-- or in a series of regularly occurring moments-- it may seem obvious to you that your partner is narcissistic. We caution you about applying this label to your partner (or to anyone) without truly understanding what it means.

To throw around labels like this can have real and negative consequences.

By all means, identify what's true for you and how you feel. Figure out what about your partner's words or actions is upsetting to you. It is far more effective to recognize that you feel ignored, for example, than to merely call your partner narcissistic.

Labels CAN be useful if applied accurately and with an intention to better understand.

#2: Get clear about what you want and need.

Recognizing your wants and needs in your relationship is essential. For the moment, focus less on what you find upsetting about your partner's habits and, instead, look at what you truly want from this relationship.

Be specific. If you feel ignored, what would it look like for you to be acknowledged and feel special in your relationship? Take out a piece of paper and a pen and write down what types of activities, conversations and experiences you'd like to share with your partner. How do you want to feel when you are together?

This isn't a demand list for you to present to your partner. It is a way for you to get clear about what your priorities are when it comes to your relationship.

#3: Create agreements with your partner.

Use your list of wants and needs to create agreements with your partner. This is not about presenting ultimatums or making threats to leave (unless you are willing actually to leave).

An agreement needs to be cooperatively reached. Make your agreements specific and ones that each of you is honestly willing to follow through with.

For example, if you feel ignored by your partner, come up with some tangible and meaningful ways that you two can make a connection-- whether it's at home, during the workday, at a party or in some other manner.

Another example of an agreement might be that you you're partner, you or both of you meet with a professional counsellor or coach who can help.

#4: **Make decisions about what's in YOUR best interests.**

Know that you get to decide what is in your best interests. A relationship is about two people coming together and honestly communicating about needs, but you are the one who ultimately chooses whether or not it's wise for you to stay in the relationship.

If your partner truly is narcissistic and refuses to do anything about it, you might decide that it is unwise for you to stay in this relationship.

Even if the "narcissist" label does not apply to your partner, you might decide that there are no indications that the improvements you seek are going to happen. You may choose to end the relationship because you believe this is an undesirable and possibly unhealthy relationship for you.

What I urge you to remember is that you get to choose. After questioning your beliefs about your partner and yourself, honestly assess whether this is the relationship you want to be in right now.

In Love with a Narcissist? Here's Some Great Relationship Advice for You!

Are you in love with someone who makes you feel like you're on a never-ending roller coaster? Is your husband, wife, boyfriend or girlfriend a bit melodramatic, constantly wanting to be at the centre of attention, a bit manipulative and acting like a spoiled brat? Are you asking yourself, is my relationship over? Then you are probably in a very tough spot -- you are in love with a narcissist. Don't go looking for breakup advice yet. Here are some classic symptoms of a narcissist, and how you can best stay in a relationship with one.

Characteristics of a Narcissist

- Often believing that they're better than others, they express disdain for others who they feel are inferior;

- They are preoccupied with power, success and attractiveness, and believe that others are jealous of them;

- They monopolize conversations and come across as conceited, boastful, or haughty;

- They exaggerate their achievements yet set unrealistic goals;

- They want constant praise and admiration;

- Appearing tough-minded, yet they are easily hurt and rejected;

- They are inconsiderate of other people's emotions and feelings;

- They often take advantage of others to the point of being exploitative.

How to Relate to a Narcissist

If you are in love with a narcissist, no doubt you have been a target of their explosive, obsessive behaviour. It is a difficult position to be in, and it's certainly easy to ask yourself if they are worth it, or when is a relationship over? As previously mentioned, it's not necessary to seek breakup advice. Here is how you can handle a narcissist.

First, give them options. Beneath their tantrums and blow-ups, narcissistic people fear being left out of the loop. What they want is to be always in control. Knowing this fact, you don't want to go to battle with them about decisions. Instead, make them feel respected and in control by offering them options to choose from, rather than bypassing their opinions and making decisions on your own. Always give them the chance to participate.

Second, have you noticed that your partner gets easily agitated when frustrated? Don't they love drama and seem to love the chaos even more? When there's a problem, direct their attention to the solution, not the details of the problem. Let them know what the challenge is, and go straight to the possible solutions. Again, this will direct their focus on the options, rather than getting them worked up about the problem! Want to make them happy? Let them grab the credit for choosing the right solution. Make them think it was their idea in the first place. If you feel uncomfortable about doing this, try it and see how the rewards you reap justify giving them the credit. People will understand - don't worry!

Lastly, go along with the ride. Now that you understand that narcissists lack empathy don't expect them to give you a lot of sympathies when you tell them your feelings, and don't expect a lot of praise from them either. Take them for who they are, and remember that they love power and truly believe they are special and unique. Since they live for attention and admiration, just praise them for their good qualities and show your delight when they do something to show their love for you.

Living with a narcissist is a mixed bag, and sometimes you might feel under-appreciated, overwhelmed, or frustrated by the relationship. But equipped with the right tools and skills, you can make it work. For more great advice about relationships, breakups and making up, please visit my website. You won't be disappointed!

CHAPTER 6

HEALING AND RECOVERING FROM NARCISSISM AND EMOTIONAL ABUSE

Discover Your Level of Narcissism

All of us have some characteristics and behaviours that fall into the category of narcissism. Narcissism is on a continuum from mild, occasional, and subtle to the more ubiquitous, obvious or extreme behaviours of a Narcissistic Personality Disorder. Since narcissism is likely a part of everyone's ego wounded self, it is helpful to your personal growth and development to be aware of your level of narcissism.

Be honest with yourself - but not judgmental - regarding the presence and intensity of the following characteristics:

I generally take others' rejecting, critical, harsh, shut-down, or diminishing behaviour personally. I tell myself that when others choose to behave in uncaring ways toward me, it is my fault - it is about me not being good enough or me doing something wrong. I make others' choices - to be open or closed, loving or unloving - about me.

I frequently judge and shame myself, trying to get myself to do things "right" so that I can have control over getting others' love, attention or approval. Getting others' love, attention and approval are vital to me.

I make others responsible for my worth, value, sense of aliveness and fullness. Others have to be kind, loving, approving of me, or sexually attracted to me, for me to feel that I'm okay. When others ignore me or are not attracted to me, I feel unworthy, depressed or empty inside.

I have a hard time having compassion for myself, so I expect others to have compassion for me when I feel anxious, depressed, angry, shamed or guilty, rather than taking responsibility for my feelings. If others lack compassion for me or criticize me, I turn things around onto them and blame them.

I lack empathy and compassion for the feelings of others, especially when I've behaved in ways that may be hurtful to others. I have a hard time recognizing or identifying with the feelings and needs of others.

When someone offers me valuable information about myself or 'tough love', I see it as an attack, rather than as a gift, and I generally attack back.

The DSM IV - The Diagnostic and Statistical Manual of Mental Disorders, states about people suffering from a Narcissistic Personality Disorder:

"Vulnerability in self-esteem makes individuals with Narcissistic Personality Disorder very sensitive to "injury" from criticism or defeat. Although they may not show it outwardly, criticism may haunt these individuals and may leave them feeling humiliated, degraded, hollow and empty. They may react with disdain, rage, or defiant counterattack. Such experience may lead to social withdrawal or an appearance of humility. Interpersonal relations are typically impaired due to problems derived from entitlement, the need for admiration, and the relative disregard for the sensitivities of others."

When in conflict with someone, or when someone behaves in a way I don't like, I often focus on getting them to deal with what they are doing, rather than focus on what I'm doing. I make them responsible for my choices and feelings, and I believe things will get better if I can get them to change.

I feel entitled to get what I want from others - whether it's money, sex, attention or approval. Others 'owe' me.

I often try to get away with things, such as not having to follow the rules or the law, and I'm indignant when I'm called to the carpet.

I see myself as special and entitled to do what I want, even if it's harmful to others.

I believe I should get credit for what I do and I should be recognized as superior, even if I do a mediocre job.

I am so unique and special that only other unique and special people can understand me. It is beneath me to associate with people who are not as special as I am. While some think I am arrogant, it is only because I'm truly so unique and special.

Because I'm so special, I have the right to demand what I want from others, and to manipulate others - with my charm, brilliance, anger or blame - into giving me what I want.

Again, all of us have some of these characteristics, and it is important to learn about them, rather than judge ourselves for them.

Narcissism can be healed. You can learn to define your worth, to give yourself the love and compassion you need to feel full inside, and to share love with others.

Healing From A Relationship With A Narcissist

Many of us have been there.

You met the person of your dreams - charming, intelligent, romantic, attentive, incredible chemistry and a great lover. You might have been told how wonderful you are, how this was the first time your lover had ever felt this way and had this level of connection, and you felt truly seen for the first time.

Perhaps there was a nagging unease that all this was happening too fast - that he or she couldn't possibly feel this way about you without knowing you better. But you were swept off your feet and finally decided to open your heart.

The confusion may have started then, as your lover pulled away and became critical. Or, it might have started after you married, and you found yourself with a partner different than the person you fell in love with.

Whether your relationship was two months or two years or two decades, it was likely tumultuous, confusing and painful. And if you were married and then divorced, it might have been more painful or even frightening.

There is much healing for you to do if you were in love with a narcissist.

The Process of Healing From Your Narcissistic Partner

1) First, you need to be very compassionate with yourself and let yourself grieve for the huge loss of what you had hoped for. It might seem easier to judge yourself for the big mistakes you believe you made, but self-judgment will keep you stuck. There is no possibility of healing when you judge yourself.

Each time the grief comes up, embrace it with kindness and caring toward yourself. Even though you know it's better to have ended this relationship; it's hard to let go of the intensity of a relationship with a narcissist. It's hard to imagine a future relationship that isn't boring compared to the intensity you've been experiencing.

2) Once some of the grief has subsided, then it's time to go inward and explore why you were vulnerable to this person. Was your partner giving you what you were not giving to yourself? Was your partner seeing you and valuing you in the way you need to be seeing and valuing

yourself? Did you ignore some red flags because you so wanted it all to be true?

Did you make excuses for your partner to avoid facing the truth? Did you give yourself up to try to have control over getting your partner to be loving to you again? What did you sacrifice to keep the relationship - your integrity, your financial security, your time with family and friends, your time for yourself, your inner knowing?

It's vitally important to be honest with yourself so that you don't end up feeling like a victim, and so that you have less of a chance of repeating this in a future relationship.

During this time of self-reflection, it's very important to get support. You might want to join a 12-Step CODA group, go into therapy/facilitation, and join a support group.

3) Educate yourself about narcissism. There are numerous books, websites and articles devoted to understanding narcissism. Since I'm certain that you don't want to repeat this, you need to do all you can to learn about what happened. You need to become sensitive to the numerous red flags so that you can pick them up very early in a subsequent relationship. I have also written several books on empathy and emotional intelligence that could be of great help to you.

One of my clients shared that she had met a man six years ago, dated him a few times, and then they remained distant friends. Recently, when she was in his town, they saw each other, and she was very attracted to him. He came on strong, inviting her to join him on an upcoming European vacation. She felt uneasy, but a day later texted him to see if he wanted to have dinner with her. He never responded to the invitation. It took her only 24 hours to recognize these two red flags of narcissism - coming on strong and then disappearing. She was pleased that she found this out so soon! Instead of beating herself up for being attracted to another narcissist, she congratulated herself for staying open to the truth.

Since narcissists are often very attractive, any of us can become attracted. But whether or not we will pursue it depends on how much Inner Bonding work we have done.

Recovery From Narcissistic Abuse - To Get Your Life Back On Track

Narcissism or Narcissistic Personality Disorder (NPD) is a mental disorder that involves a persistent pattern of grandiosity. The person with this disorder constantly wants to be admired, is obsessed and infatuated with himself. The narcissistic individual also lacks compassion and empathy; is ruthless, egotistical, seeking dominance and gratification. To deal with and to live with a narcissistic can leave someone very traumatized due to the emotional abuse the narcissistic partner has caused. If you were married to a narcissist, you might find that it is difficult to escape from that relationship. If you do escape, your recovery will be long and painful. No matter how difficult the road to recovery is, you have to get through it so that your life will be back on track again.

- You have to know what the qualities of a narcissistic person are. It would include a frequent display of jealousy, infidelity, control, lying, and insecurity, verbal and even physical abuse. If these behaviours are not excused and are often tolerated, it would seem to the narcissistic person that they are acceptable. If you were successful in leaving a narcissistic partner or spouse, he would certainly lure you back again. As much as you love this person, you have to be firm in letting him know that his narcissistic behaviour may only be resolved with the help of a professional. He must seek professional assistance to correct his abusive personality, or he will not change. Being manipulated and believing that your ex will change on his own accord will only bring you back to a miserable and painful life.

- In recovering, you also need to realize that you are your complete person. When you decided to be in a relationship or marry a narcissistic person, you may have already developed a dependency on that person. He may have captured your heart with his attentive, generous and suave personality. This then resulted in your emotional dependency on him that eventually turned out as something for you to regret. Once escaped from the binding relationship with a narcissist, do your best to regain your emotional independence. It will help you to be firm and able to stand again on your own. Learn to love and accept your self-worth. Set your standards for whoever will soon come into your life. Do not accept anyone whose attributes are less than the standards you have set and you know you rightfully deserve.

- You may also look for groups and organizations where you can be a part of. These groups offer help and an opportunity to communicate and interact with other people who have suffered and endured narcissistic relationships. These are the people whom you need to be with, together you can inspire one another and help one another obtain complete recovery and freedom from your experience.

Emotional Abuse - 8 Steps to Recovery

Do you remember the day your partner left you for someone new? That sick sinking feeling in your gut that you just weren't good enough? You tried so hard, and in the end, she was gone and with someone new.

At first, the silence was deafening, and you were so lonely, so very lonely. How could she be in love with you one day and love with someone else the next? You called. You texted. You just needed answers, but never got any response. You wanted a second chance to prove you could be better, but after a while, this passed, too, and you thought you were going to finally make it through the heartache.

You decide you don't want anything more to do with her and stop trying to contact her. BUT, now all those emotions are flooding back, and you just want to cry out in frustration after getting ANOTHER text, call or email from your ex. She hasn't heard from you in a while and misses you. She wants to get together, and so you do. She never really explains why she cheated or why she came back.

She's just back, and you are on cloud nine... for a few months. Then the same thing happens again.

And here you are again, alone and still in love with the same person who "claimed" the breakup was your fault, that you weren't good enough. She's again ignoring your calls and texts wanting an explanation for why she walked out? The same person who was just posting all over Facebook about the "new" love in her life? And just like before, once you start to come out of the fog and start thinking it's over, all of a sudden, she wants you back? Do you feel trapped in a never-ending cycle of abuse, like a washing machine - rinse, spin, repeat, rinse, spin, repeat.

When you are together, does she make you feel like you are walking on eggshells, praying you don't do anything to upset her? Do you ignore or avoid calling her out on the hurtful things she says or does because you fear that every argument is your last? Does she constantly put you down and make you feel inferior to her? Have you stopped speaking to family and friends since you two have been together?

Wasn't this the same person who called you her soul mate? Do you remember she talked about her ex when you first got together? How crazy and jealous her ex was, and how glad she was to have found you. She told you that you were her soul mate.

Do you fall for her lies again, thinking you can recapture the early period of your relationship, when she was good and caring and kind? I don't like being the bearer of bad news, but I have to tell you, you're in relationship hell, stuck on a roller coaster, and to save yourself, you have to get away from this narcopath, who is nothing more than an emotional vampire.

Here's some hard-learned information. When you are desperately texting and calling to get "closure" by having your questions answered, you are feeding her energy. She thrives on this behaviour from you. It makes her feel powerful. She loves telling her new flame and all her friends how crazy psycho you are now. But, when you finally realize it's over, and stop calling and texting, guess what? She's not getting that supply of energy she is addicted to so much, and she thinks she's about to lose a great source of supply, so she starts calling and texting you. KNOW THIS: No normal person truly in love does this sort of thing. She is hovering - a term used to describe a narcopath who feels like you may be slipping away from her death grip.

It's imperative that you have no contact with this person. Even when she plays on your guilt or uses shame to trick you into "just talking to her", don't fall for it. Make yourself think like she thinks when you are dealing with her. She has no conscience or qualms about hurting you, so you take on the same attitude. It will continue, and the no contact may very well send her into a narcissistic rage. It doesn't matter what she does, stick to no contact.

In recovering from the emotional and verbal abuse of your former partner, here are eight steps you need to take to prepare yourself not to break the no contact rule:

1. Recognize that your love for this person is REAL. Ignoring this fact only sets you up for more abuse;

2. Recognize that this person lied to you, tricked you into falling in love. Think about it for a second. Had you met the person you are with now, would you have gone on a second date? Hell, no. It was an act, only an act. A narcopath is incapable of experiencing real emotion like love, empathy, compassion, guilt, etc. The only emotion I believe they feel is anger, and I'm sure you've seen the irrational rage common with narcopaths;

3. Accept the fact you will never get the answers to the burning questions you have;

4. Accept that the dream she promised was a lie;

5. Accept the fact that you can only change yourself, you cannot change her, and despite promises of change she always makes to get you to come back, she will not change;

6. Once you have internalized the first four steps, then you are ready to commit yourself to have absolutely no contact with her whatsoever. If you have children together, then limit the contact to ONLY discussions about the children;

7. Find a therapist to talk to. If you aren't comfortable talking to anyone face-to-face, then join a members-only site that offers advice and counselling; and finally

8. Find activities that help you restore your self-worth, your self-confidence and your joy. Colour therapy is an excellent activity for opening up your mind to new ideas

and focusing on colouring puts you in a positive state of mind. EBT is good if you understand how it's done.

Best Tips to Recover From Narcissistic Abuse

How to heal from emotional abuse starts by recognizing that you have a problem. Even if you have already severed ties from an abusive relationship, it doesn't mean that everything will just go back to being alright.

There is an invisible energy stream that still exists between you and your previous abusive partner. It prevents you from being able to move forward with your life as you still unconsciously carry the emotional burden caused by the narcissist. You need to actively work from separating yourself in mind and soul to be able to break free from it. You will soon learn how as you continue to read along.

It is very helpful to regard yourself as a survivor and a winner instead of a victim. It immediately empowers you and gives you back control of your life. Here are some tips on how to heal from emotional abuse:

Understand that it's not your fault

Once you can find comfort in the fact that it's not your fault, you will begin to realize that you are not the cause of negative experiences you have gone through as opposed to what your abuser made you believe.

Confide in a close friend or relative

The people you trust will be able to provide you with the love and support at this critical time of healing. Talking about what you have gone through will help you better understand and accept your experience of abuse.

Discover coping tools

Find out what helps you express your emotions, release anger or grief. Writing in a journal, composing poems or songs, painting, any sport or playing a musical instrument can help you cope and let out your feelings. It will aid you in taking your mind off the pain you suffered and replace it with good and happy memories.

Take care of yourself

Learn to look after yourself first before taking care of others. Believe that you are worthy of respect, love and acceptance just like everybody else. Take pride in your unique qualities and improve on your weaknesses. You have to have faith in yourself first before other people do.

www.ingramcontent.com/pod-product-compliance
Lightning Source LLC
Chambersburg PA
CBHW070919080526
44589CB00013B/1362